The New Six Sigma ®

A Leader's ...
Rapid Busi... ...
and Susta... ... *Results*

Matt Barney and Tom McCarty

**MOTOROLA
UNIVERSITY**

PRENTICE
HALL
PTR
Prentice Hall PTR
Professional Technical Reference
Upper Saddle River, NJ 07458
www.phptr.com

ISBN 0-13-101399-8

9 780131 013995

9 1595

Library of Congress Cataloging in Publication Data:

The new Six Sigma : a leader's guide to achieving rapid business improvement and sustainable results / Matt Barney & Tom McCarty, eds.
     p.   cm
    Includes bibilographical references and index.
    ISBN 0-13-101399-8
    1. Total quality management. 2. Six sigma (Quality control standard) 3. Leadership. I. Barney, Matt. II. McCarty, Tom.
HD62.15.N48 2003
658.4'013--dc21

                                      2002034373

Editorial/Production Supervision: *Donna Cullen-Dolce*
Publisher: *Bernard Goodwin*
Cover Design Director: *Jerry Votta*
Cover Design: *Nina Scuderi*
Manufacturing Manager: *Maura Zaldivar*
Marketing Manager: *Dan DePasquale*
Editorial Assistant: *Michele Vincenti*

© 2003 Pearson Education
Publishing as Prentice Hall PTR
Upper Saddle River, NJ 07458

PRENTICE
HALL
PTR

Prentice Hall books are widely used by corporations and government agencies for training, marketing, and resale.

For information regarding corporate and government bulk discounts please contact: Corporate and Government Sales (800) 382-3419 or corpsales@pearsontechgroup.com

Or write: Prentice Hall PTR, Corporate Sales Dept., One Lake Street, Upper Saddle River, NJ 07458.

Six Sigma is a registered trademark of Motorola Corporation.

Other company and product names mentioned herein are the trademarks or registered trademarks of their respective owners.

Printed in the United States of America

10 9 8 7 6 5 4 3 2

ISBN 0-13-101399-8

Pearson Education LTD.
Pearson Education Australia PTY, Limited
Pearson Education Singapore, Pte. Ltd.
Pearson Education North Asia Ltd.
Pearson Education Canada, Ltd.
Pearson Educación de Mexico, S.A. de C.V.
Pearson Education—Japan
Pearson Education Malaysia, Pte. Ltd.

Contents

Chapter 4

Thoughts About the New Six Sigma

by Gary Cone

I have had the privilege of observing from the inside several of the most highly regarded companies and business leaders of the late 20th and early 21st century. Motorola and Bob Galvin, Compaq Computers and Rod Canion, AlliedSignal and Larry Bossidy, and General Electric and Jack Welch comprise my list. Not bad. All were extraordinarily exciting places to work at a point in time, but none compared with working at Motorola's Automotive and Industrial Electronics Group (AIEG) in the late 1980s and early 1990s.

I often worked 18-hour days. I moved a factory from Building 1299 in Chicago while living in Buffalo. I built a factory for a customer in Milano, Italy, while living in Chicago. I took an assignment driving better-quality systems, cycle-time reduction, and Six Sigma in such far-flung places as Taiwan, Italy, France, and England, and as close to home as New York, Texas, and Illinois. I spent my life on airplanes and in hotels, and my shoulder still aches from the 25-pound Zenith Data Systems "laptop" I carried so I could use Lotus 123 to do simple simulations and a DOS version of Minitab for statistical analysis. It was the most fun I ever had.

I have taken some time to reflect on why this was so. Compaq was a miserable place for me to work. It was "world class" but losing money and market share. The company was certain there was nothing to learn. At Zenith Data Systems, I was a vice-president, and I couldn't stand it. At the time, Zenith was the third-largest PC supplier in the world and an innovator in the PC world (this is a fact—first laptop, first notebook, first integrated Ethernet as a standard), but it could not hit market windows. The company was proud of the innovation and saw no need to learn.

What was different? Did I throw away the best job in the world when I left Motorola? I certainly thought about it.

Let's look at a few of the specifics. . .

• ***Building the customer's factory***—The customer had its back against the wall. The European Union had mandated fuel injection in all cars in less than a year and a half, and although the customer had a product, the manufacturing cycle was long (about three days), the yield was low, the product was going through a 24-hour burn-in, and the field reliability was poor (about 2 percent failures per month!). The customer had the opportunity to own the southern European market for fuel injection, but most of its customers were considering Bosch because of the problems. The deal was that Motorola could have 50 percent of its fuel injection electronics business (there is a lot to fuel injection besides the electronics) if we could help the customer design the right product, design the right process, and implement both with its people. I had so much faith in the methodology that I thought we could do this in a foreign country in a factory not owned or managed by Motorola. Motorola again allowed me to take one person (Karl Werwath, a brilliant process manager that I had sense enough to stay out of his way). We launched a product in 13 months, one month early, which required no burn-in and had a Sigma level equal to our best product in Seguin, Texas—our best factory. The process we followed is now referred to as Design for Six Sigma; it was the collaborative work of a team of design engineers in Chicago and Torino, and a team of process engineers in Seguin, Angers, and Pavia. We were having fun. We were learning.

• *AlliedSignal*—I was responsible for its Six Sigma deployment within the automotive sector, a $6 billion business. AlliedSignal made such things as seat belts, air bags, brake pads, air brakes for trucks, turbo chargers, spark plugs, and oil filters; my prior experience and our examples were about silicon wafers and electronics assemblies. We no longer had the safety net of Motorola University, and our intellectual property was unusable. Larry Bossidy expected results. I was teaching six Black Belt classes per year with 35–40 people in each class. With the aid of Steve Zinkgraf, we were creating intellectual property on a just-in-time basis. We were following the action learning model we learned at Motorola. We had tremendous results. We were having fun. We were learning.

- *GE*—It wanted 70 percent of all projects in nonmanufacturing areas! Although we had several examples of the techniques working outside of manufacturing, and we all knew it would work, 70 percent? Wow, what a stretch. Jack Welch expected results. The GE folks figured it out. They have the Baskin Robbins of Six Sigma, there are so many flavors, and I lost count years ago. Black Belt/Green Belt may have many different meanings and intellectual properties, but they all work. What is the common thread? They were all driven by a common vision and a common set of metrics (just like Motorola AIEG). They were having fun. They were learning.

For me, Six Sigma has been mundane since those first heady years of GE and AlliedSignal. What a wild time. All professionals get at least Green Belt training. No one gets promoted without being certified in Six Sigma. Going after billions of dollars in savings per year! Jack and Larry were wild men, and they got what they asked for—and measured and rewarded. And they were just following the example of the real visionary— Bob Galvin. They did not do anything Bob hadn't done, they just did it bigger, with a tad more flair, to an audience of Wall Street analysts. Since then, it is just a lot of "I want to be like Jack." The method has stagnated and has been compromised to a great extent by the services offered by many providers:

Black Belts in two weeks, no, wait—one week!

Black Belts with no training, just an affidavit and a test

Standalone Web-based training for Green Belt and Black Belt

Everyone claiming to be a Master Black Belt

I can count on my hands and feet the number of Master Black Belts with more than five years of experience. Everyone is expecting huge pay increases after being trained in basic process discipline by his or her employer! Too many expect to achieve results like GE by hiring a former GE Black Belt or Green Belt. There are a lot of disappointed people.

Let's stop the insanity. There is no net gain in intellectual property from taking shortcuts. You can't be like Jack; you have to become your own leader. You are not a genius because Six Sigma is bringing results in your somewhat-unique niche. Disciplined, structured logical techniques, along with knowledge sharing with coaches, and measurement will bring positive results. The results are enhanced if management steps up and supports its people. The results are even better if management breaks down barriers and creates a culture where it is unacceptable to have process knowledge and not share it. The results are phenomenal if the work is focused in areas that are important to the paying customer.

The New Six Sigma delivers three things:

1. **An accurate accounting of the history of Six Sigma**—Thank God, now maybe we can dismiss all of the nonsense that is out there. I would just remind all of the current leaders at Motorola to respect the courage of all those who believed and adopted and learned and pushed the envelope. They had fun and would not trade the experience, but they were (and are) working without a net.

2. **A clear articulation of the role of leadership**— Tom McCarty describes the framework that enables Six Sigma better than I have ever seen. His section on Six Sigma's present, along with *Adhocracy*, by Bob Waterman, should be required reading for all leaders and all MBA students. It is what Larry, Jack, and most importantly Bob Galvin knew. Leaders— embrace Align, Mobilize, Accelerate, and Govern, or you will fail. Most of what is being called Six Sigma today does not comprehend this, and those efforts lack relevance just like most TQM efforts. If you are unclear whether I'm referring to you, ask your employees. Given the chance, they will be honest with you.

3. **A roadmap and leadership to take Six Sigma to the next step**—Motorola knows it starts by embracing and nurturing leadership. Six Sigma never was about stagnation or learning to apply technology, although certain things like statistical software for PCs and knowledge-sharing networks are really useful. This is about sharing what you know, considering and trying what you have not yet used, and gaining great satisfaction from others taking it further than you ever envisioned. I've often described this as "tools usable and used." Tools come into the

toolset when they demonstrate their usefulness. Matt Barney has proposed usable tools. Now it's up to the leading-edge practitioners to demonstrate their use.

The learning has awakened from a slumber. Motorola is reclaiming the lead with a clear objective of not losing its way. It is under no delusion that this cannot happen.

This book should be called *The Real Six Sigma*.

Let the fun begin.

Gary Cone
President & CEO,
Global Productivity Solutions

Preface

Six Sigma has come a long way from its roots as a way to reduce defects.

Motorola recently improved traditional Six Sigma techniques and successfully applied them in many different types of organizations around the world. As Six Sigma's inventor, Motorola is uniquely qualified to provide insight into past failures and future opportunities. This book is the first to outline the innovations and improvements made to Six Sigma.

The New Six Sigma is organized around a time principle—the past, present, and future of Six Sigma. We start with a brief review of Six Sigma's origins, highlighting the lessons Motorola learned through experience. This background sets the stage for the core of the book—an introduction to the New Six Sigma. In its classical form, Six Sigma has been used extensively to improve product quality, mostly in manufacturing settings. Motorola built on these beginnings and reinvented Six Sigma to move beyond defects and focus more on strategy execution and value creation. The redesigned and refocused Six Sigma retains its analytical and project management tools, but these tools have been redirected toward strategic business improvement. We've applied these innovations both within Motorola and externally, with our customers and suppliers, to ensure impact on a wide range of service, business, and government organizations. The New Six Sigma is a leadership governance process that improves business results in all parts of a firm. In our final section, we show where Six Sigma is headed. We first document the cutting-edge practices recently implemented in Motorola's Leadership Supply processes, and we end with a look at innovative ideas for the future of Six Sigma. These ideas range from improving financial accounting, to improving the assessment of customer requirements, through sophisticated tangible and intangible asset management techniques.

Motorola has built on Six Sigma's powerful past, and the future looks very bright.

ACKNOWLEDGMENTS

We wish to thank a number of important people who contributed to this work. First, the support of Sandy Ogg, Augie

Rojas, and Jamie Lane made this book possible. We also thank Ed Bales, Carey Dassatti, and Alejandro Reyes for authoring portions of this book, and we appreciate the input of Susan Shinn and Bernard Goodwin, who shared their expertise about the publishing process. Lastly, we thank our families—the McCarty's and Sarkar-Barney's—for their support.

Chapter 1

Six Sigma— The Past

by Ed Bales

HISTORY OF SIX SIGMA

By the early 1970s, Motorola had established itself as the world leader in wireless communications products, and it was battling Texas Instruments and Intel for the number one slot in semiconductor sales. In 1974, five of the top eight semiconductor manufacturers were American and three were European. But competition in the semiconductor market soon grew very fierce. Just five years later, in 1979, two of the top eight chip manufacturers were Japanese. The Japanese were also beginning to erode Motorola's lead in the U.S. paging market.

These difficulties were prefigured in 1973, when Motorola, finding itself unable to compete in the consumer products market, sold its consumer electronics division to a Japanese company. The threat to the company's future was clearly on the horizon; nevertheless, a majority of Motorola's senior leaders ignored the warning signs.

In 1979, under the leadership of CEO Bob Galvin, a task force began to develop a plan for Motorola's renewal and growth. This work accelerated after Art Sundry, the most senior sales vice-president of the largest communications group, shouted "Our quality stinks" in the May 1979 officers meeting. Sundry's outburst resulted from feedback he received from customers and users of Motorola's communications products. Together, Galvin's task force and Sundry's research led to the creation of a four-point plan, rolled out in 1980, with the aim of securing Motorola's global leadership:

1. **Global competitiveness**—Ensuring market and product superiority by benchmarking the company against global competitors; designing products for global distribution; and breaking down trade barriers that kept Motorola products out of Japan and other international markets.

2. **Participative management**—Drawing on traditional Total Quality Management (TQM) philosophy to adapt the principals and methodology of quality circles to the Motorola culture; sharing profit improvements with all employees.

3. **Quality improvements**—Establishing goals of improving quality tenfold (10X) within five years and placing quality improvement goals in the incentive

packages of all executives; this initiative sowed the seeds of Six Sigma.

4. **Motorola Training and Education Center—** Creating the precursor to Motorola University, which addressed the fact that the dramatic changes required in quality processes and management style would create a great incompetence in the work-force—not because of workers' unintelligence, but due to the insufficient information they received on how to meet the new job requirements.

Galvin selected senior executives to drive each of these four initiatives and had them report directly to his office.

The 10X quality improvement goal drove significant change in each of the business units. However, at this time, quality improvement efforts were focused exclusively on the manufacturing function because conventional wisdom dictated that manufacturing was the source of a majority of the problems and held the greatest promise for improvement.

Based on this premise, the company established the Motorola Manufacturing Institute (MMI) in 1984 under the direction of a senior manufacturing vice-president, Carlton Braun. This two-week program for senior manufacturing managers focused on developing and sharing quality improvement goals. In providing feedback, the first groups of managers who completed the program commented that the 10X quality improvement goal could never be achieved by focusing on the manufacturing function alone. Managers were convinced that all functions needed to be involved, particularly engineering design. These remarks resulted in improved courses and the refocus of the institute away from just manufacturing and toward all aspects of management.

Consequently, the institute, renamed the Motorola Management Institute, represented all business functions in every class. This institute served as a major catalyst in breaking down the silos that existed between functions. Quality improvements along with cost and cycle-time reductions could only be achieved through the involvement of all who impacted or were impacted by the development of new Motorola products and services. As a result, customers and suppliers began to get involved in the design of next-generation products. This part of Six Sigma's history reflects Motorola's earliest realization that all parts of the business impact the achievement of strategic outcomes and all efforts must be aligned toward improving results in order to reach the goals of improved quality and customer satisfaction.

Motorola still lacked a common metric for sharing and comparing improvement initiatives, and this deficiency served as a major barrier to alignment. Then, in late 1985, quality engineer Bill Smith, frustrated by his associate's rejection of his quality measurement ideas, scheduled a meeting with Bob Galvin. After listening to Smith's point of view, Galvin instructed Jack Germain, the corporate vice-president of Quality, to build on Smith's ideas.

As a result, Smith and a team of quality managers created a three-day program entitled "Design for Manufacturability" (DFM). Facilitated by a Motorola University designer, Ann Dille, DFM defined the "Six Steps to Six Sigma" and became the first required training program for all technical personnel worldwide. Another

Motorola engineer, Craig Fullerton, developed and taught "Six Sigma Design Methodology" (SSDM—today called Design for Six Sigma, or DFSS, by most other companies). The Six Sigma Design Methodology focused on ensuring winning product design. Six Sigma now aligned all quality efforts around a common measurement process, and Six Sigma goals drove every team worldwide. Six Sigma's success led Motorola's managers to set an even more aggressive goal, from 10X to 100X improvement.

Participants in the initial implementation of the DFM program felt that all functions and not just the technical employees needed to use the Six Sigma methodology. A one-day course entitled "Understanding Six Sigma" was then developed for all nontechnical employees worldwide, and Motorolans began to use Six Sigma on everything from measuring training defects to financial effectiveness. At this point, Motorola had two of the major components of continuous improvement in place. All quality improvement efforts were now *aligned* around the concepts of Six Sigma, and all employees were *mobilized* by common Six Sigma goals and reward systems.

These efforts resulted in Motorola receiving the first Malcolm Baldrige National Quality Award from the U.S Government in 1988. In describing the corporation's renewal, one of the Malcolm Baldrige auditors commented that wherever he went and whomever he talked to, the Six Sigma concept was articulated and understood. The alignment of the culture around the quality goal had been achieved.

Six Sigma began as an initiative for improving quality rather than as a methodology for continuous business improvement. Once organizations achieved the Six Sigma goal, they stopped improving—they became "good enough." This mindset caused complacency that allowed quality to actually deteriorate.

By 1990, Motorola was struggling to reach Six Sigma in everything it did, yet it seemed to be stuck at 5.4 Sigma. Bill Wiggenhorn, president of Motorola University, proposed the establishment of a Six Sigma Research Institute (SSRI) to bring leading engineers and statisticians together with the goal of finding new ways to *accelerate* the achievement of "Six Sigma and Beyond." The SSRI became an alliance of IBM, Texas Instruments, Kodak, and others, all of which provided resources that drove the search for new quality improvement ideas. These efforts resulted in the adoption of new and powerful software tools required to analyze the large amounts of data generated by Six Sigma projects. The foundation of this work was a focus on the root cause of the problem and a reduction of sources of variability. Another key concept—that of the "Black Belt"—resulted from the SSRI.

A team of improvement experts from the SSRI companies, led by Motorola statistician Harrison "Skip" Weed, Ph.D., defined the first content and standards for a Black Belt based on concepts that originated with Motorola's statistical experts in Asia. Black Belts were originally intended to be improvement experts that led teams to ensure a high probability of success. But Weed's team decided that to achieve Black Belt recognition, candidates must demonstrate statistical, team, and business skill along with business impact. The output of the SSRI Black Belt work was shared with both the original companies in the alliance and non-alliance companies, and General Electric became one of the first non-alliance members to internalize the Six Sigma methodology. By this stage of Six Sigma's evolution, Motorola had successfully germinated three of the four major components of the business improvement model it nurtured into the model used today—the concepts of Alignment with business goals, Mobilizing teams, and Accelerating the speed to results.

To further institutionalize and accelerate the new culture of improvement, Motorola built new business processes and adopted a new learning standard. "Action learning" became the model for senior executive development and later Black Belt training. Teams of top executives were brought together to focus on critical issues (e.g., software development quality and moving into emerging markets). Motorola University designed and facilitated these executive meetings, during which participants gained new knowledge about the focus topic. The CEO directed executives to apply the new knowledge to their businesses and share this action learning with other businesses.

This process of "learning-action-feedback" accelerated change at an unprecedented rate, moving into the business units through the development of Total Customer Satisfaction (TCS) teams. Thousands of TCS teams were formed at every level to address problems in the workplace. These teams would pull together the people and resources necessary to improve the quality of the work in manufacturing, engineering, human resources, finance, and all other functions. TCS teams shared their results globally so that new learning taking place in one part of the world could be duplicated elsewhere. The development of the Six Sigma Black Belt Steering Committee, the Corporate Quality Steering Committee, and a global process of Quality System Reviews (QSR) further drove the institutionalization of the quality culture.

Motorola had learned that maintaining and even going beyond Six Sigma required strong leadership committed to the development and implementation of process: Alignment, Mobilization, Acceleration, and Governance. These concepts facilitate the creation of new cultures or the changing of existing ones within and across all business functions. Continuous improvement requires continuous change, which in turn requires continuous learning. Motorola University succeeded as a catalyst for continuous learning, and it proved that without refreshing and updating skills, improvement is not possible. Learning is at the heart of continuously improving quality and other important business results.

Chapter 2

Six Sigma— The Present

by Tom McCarty

In the first years of the 21st century, leaders face a new reality. We must consistently generate positive, month-to-month financial results while continuously building a business that will sustain those results over the longer term. While balancing short term and long term has always concerned executives, today's environment demands performance along both dimensions. Fierce new competitors, demanding customers, tight talent supplies, and wildly fluctuating markets are a reality in almost every industry; meanwhile, investors show no willingness to wait for returns on their investments.

Executives attempting to chart a course through these waters feel schizophrenic and myopic. They work to answer weekly demands for an improved financial picture while trying to communicate a long-term vision and roadmap to customers, suppliers, and employees. Management approaches that have been successful in the past are no longer effective. Fortunately, in every industry there are executives who outperform their peers.

For the past few years, Motorola University has worked to understand what differentiates top-performing executive teams, both inside Motorola and across many industries. Remarkably, we've discovered important parallels between our findings and lessons from Six Sigma's past. Top-performing leadership teams demonstrate a keen sense of daily priorities. They also possess the ability to effectively execute those priorities while still maintaining a compelling vision for the future, and this enables others to act on that vision. Furthermore, top teams always operate ethically. To leverage these personal attributes, many executives have adopted common best practices that give them an edge in creating a vision, establishing priorities, enabling people to take action, and driving execution in a way that satisfies short-term demands while building capability for future growth. These best practices have been documented and incorporated into an approach to executive management and leadership that is the New Six Sigma.

> The old Six Sigma was just a standard measure of goodness.

INTRODUCTION TO THE NEW SIX SIGMA

Motorola University developed the New Six Sigma because we had to. We could see our Motorola businesses as well as our customers and suppliers struggling with the same critical issues. We knew that the classic Six Sigma methodology—focus on defects and variability reduction—had served our business managers quite effectively during much of the 1990s, and we had helped our customers and suppliers apply Six Sigma to dramatically improve their business processes. But we could also see that Six Sigma was losing its relevance to many of our business leaders. They perceived the methodology as too complex, effective only in manufacturing and engineering environments, and too slow in yielding results. We could also see, however, that many of our leaders had taken the important elements of Six Sigma—like understanding customer requirements, continuously driving process improvement, and using statistical analysis to drive fact-based decision making—and moved them into a broader, integrated approach that flawlessly executed their full business strategies. The New Six Sigma builds on the power of the Six Sigma methodology we pioneered in the 1980s and introduced to many businesses in the 1990s, yet it benefits from the lessons we learned as we helped our customers and suppliers implement the methodology.

> The new Six Sigma is an overall business improvement method.

The New Six Sigma solves the paradox that leaders find themselves in today of attempting to simultaneously achieve short-term financial gains through fast business improvement projects while building future capability in both key talent and critical processes.

By integrating tools and processes such as scorecards, business process redesign, high-performance teams, and continuous monitoring of key business metrics, the New Six Sigma provides a practical approach and useful tools for leaders looking to drive balanced execution.

Table 2.1 outlines the four key leadership principles, discerned through studying organizations that successfully implemented Six Sigma. These leadership principles anchor the New Six Sigma.1

The New Six Sigma integrates best-practice processes with tools designed to help leaders in driving their business strategy for dramatic short-term business results while building sustained future capability.

Table 2.1 Leadership Principles of the New Six Sigma

Key Leadership Principle	Description
Align	• Using the performance excellence business model (based on the Malcolm Baldrige criteria), link customer requirements to business strategy and core business processes. • Create strategy execution targets, stretch goals, and appropriate measures. The goal is to provide sustainable, measurable bottom-line results that drive business goal achievement.
Mobilize	• Empower teams to drive improvements using projects selected by executives, project management methodology, and Six Sigma methods. • Organize team efforts with clear charters, success criteria, and rigorous reviews. • Provide teams with just-in-time training and empower them to act.
Accelerate	• Employ an action learning methodology by combining structured education with real-time project work and coaching to quickly bridge the gap from *learning* to *doing*. The motivation to act is perishable yet essential for driving projects to timely results.
Govern	• Drive the execution of strategy by managing scorecard metrics. Structured review processes involve reviewing dashboards of results as well as drilling into process and project details where needed. Barriers lift when leaders share best practices.

Table 2.2 shows some of the best practices that were
included in the New Six Sigma methodology.

Table 2.2 *Best Practices of the New*
Six Sigma

Best Practice Process or Tool	Definition or Purpose
Voice of the Customer (VOC)	Six Sigma methods translate abstract desires from customers into concrete specifications and organizational requirements. Leaders use these data to transform the strategic goals and processes so that they deliver value.
Balanced Scorecard	Executive teams actively build scorecards to quickly achieve alignment on their organization's vision, mission, strategic objectives, breakthrough initiatives, and the metrics used for monitoring progress. The scorecard itself provides the vehicle for clear and concise communication of vision, mission, objectives, metrics, and initiatives to the entire organization.
Accelerated Business Improvement	Business process redesign provides the tools that enable the creation or redesign of the key business processes essential for delivering on the customer's expectations and achieving the goals articulated in the scorecard.

Table 2.2   Best Practices of the New Six Sigma (Continued)

Best Practice Process or Tool	Definition or Purpose
High-Performance Teams	High-performance teams are customer-focused, cross-functional teams with clear charters used to complete the projects most critical to the business improvement effort.

Six Sigma Black Belt Teams	Six Sigma Black Belt teams are:
	• Employed against highly complex projects that require advanced statistical tools.
	• Used when an advanced tool set is required to achieve:
	  • Process improvement.
	  • Process development.
	  • Product or service improvement.
	  • Product or service development.

Blitz Teams	Blitz Teams are employed when: • It's clear what needs to improve. • Detailed data analysis is not required. • The consequences of not taking action outweigh the risks of making mistakes. • Leaders are ready to support action.
Integrated Business Review	Executives use a dashboard—a summary of the status of metrics—to review the progress toward goals. Leaders drill into details when stoplights on the dashboard indicate unfavorable trends or goals. Details include process status and projects that aim to improve processes.

The next section uses the New Six Sigma methodology to provide leaders with a practical approach to achieving rapid business improvement while building sustainability into their business systems. It builds leaders' understanding of the four key insights (Align, Mobilize, Accelerate, Govern), and it guides them through the use of New Six Sigma practices and tools by providing real-world examples.

To clarify these concepts, we have combined Motorola's experiences with those of the many other companies who have practiced the New Six Sigma over the past few years. The case study that follows demonstrates how novel leadership principles and innovations make the New Six Sigma significantly better than the original.

THE NEW SIX SIGMA IN ACTION— A CASE STUDY

Ron Brown is the general manager of a fully integrated business unit responsible for the development, production, and sales of products and services used in high-tech electronics applications. Ron recently replaced a general manager who had been managing the business for the past 10 years, and he found himself facing a number of challenges.

With a solid reputation as technology wizards, Apex and its employees built their success on a formula of one new technology breakthrough after another. As a result, Apex has sustained a 20 percent growth rate for the past 10 years. But after 10 years of growth, Apex customers have lost their appetite for investment in speculative technologies; they are demanding more performance at a lower price and more responsive service on currently installed products and systems. New competitors are finding ways to copy Apex products and deliver them at a lower price. As customer order rates dramatically decline, inventories quickly build, and Apex is finding it difficult to reduce product costs or attract new customers for its higher margin products. Cash flow is suffering, and Apex cannot fund new product development opportunities the way it had in the past. Needless to say, Ron is not sleeping very well these days.

Ron had noticed stories about companies like Motorola, GE, and Caterpillar that turned their businesses around with Six Sigma, and he wondered if the Six Sigma methodology could be applied to his situation. For assistance in applying Six Sigma, Ron went directly to the folks who invented and refined the methodology—Motorola University. He sought us out because of our experience, and he found it encouraging that we had faced situations similar to his in the same markets. He also liked that Motorola, unlike a consulting firm that gives advice it doesn't use, lives and breathes the methods we recommend to others. During a visit to Motorola University, Ron learned about how New Six Sigma techniques have dramatically turned around businesses just like his; as a result, he decided to enlist the Motorola University consulting services in his business improvement campaign.

Ron felt excited but apprehensive when he called a staff meeting to secure sponsorship support for the launch of the Apex Six Sigma business improvement campaign. He quickly found that staff members did not share his enthusiasm. Harold, the vice-president of

Engineering, was no stranger to Six Sigma; he related the fact that, while he had successfully applied Six Sigma in several production areas, it seemed too complicated to some. He mistakenly thought it required a Ph.D. in Statistics to successfully implement. Harold's experience was that a Six Sigma project could tie up a team for six months with no certainty that the fix would be sustainable.

Barbara, the vice-president of Human Resources, voiced concern about the effect another initiative would have on employees' morale. Already experiencing initiative overload, employees were spread too thin with various team assignments. While Mary, the vice-president of Sales, was happy to hear that the engineers might finally clean up their product quality problems, she didn't feel that Six Sigma would do anything to boost her sales force's productivity. She had already invested too much in sales automation and customer resource management tools, and was patiently waiting to see a return on those investments. Mary also felt that Six Sigma, like other cost-reduction initiatives, could deflect attention from her efforts to improve overall customer satisfaction. Finally, Jack, the chief financial officer, expressed his reservations. He had seen too many dollars invested in total quality management programs that got organizations all whipped up with quality rhetoric while financial results continued to decline. In his view, Apex didn't have time to run another program—it simply needed to solve its obvious problems within the next 90 days.

Ron wanted to deal with these perceptions before moving forward, so he took out a flip chart and listed the concerns that had been expressed. He then countered with what he had learned about ways the New Six Sigma methodology could address these issues (Table 2.3).

Table 2.3   *Ways the New Six Sigma Addresses Common Concerns*

Common Misperceptions about Six Sigma	The New Six Sigma Approach
Six Sigma only applies in a manufacturing environment.	Six Sigma provides tools that enable teams to improve any type of process, both continuous and transactional.
Six Sigma is too complicated and requires a Ph.D. in Statistics.	Breakthroughs in desktop software and improved courseware enable teams to complete complex analysis and experiments quickly and easily.
Six Sigma projects can go on for months with no clear gains assured.	Clear project charters, upfront financial benefits analysis, and executive accountability ensure timely completion of projects as well as significant financial returns on every project.
Six Sigma projects add to employee overload.	Project prioritization and continuous management review ensure the optimization of team resources.
Six Sigma primarily focuses on cost reduction.	While cost reduction is usually an important outcome, all projects first focus on meeting critical customer requirements.

Table 2.3 *Ways the New Six Sigma Addresses Common Concerns (Continued)*

Common Misperceptions about Six Sigma	The New Six Sigma Approach
Six Sigma programs create more "initiative of the month" confusion.	Six Sigma can be the integrating force that brings current initiatives into alignment and focuses all initiatives on breakthrough business improvement.
Six Sigma is just another name for TQM.	While Six Sigma utilizes many TQM tools, these tools are applied for breakthrough business improvement and sustainable financial returns.
Six Sigma requires heavy investment, with no clear line of sight to return on investment.	Investments in Six Sigma projects are accretive—all projects are selected based on their ability to achieve clear return-on-investment goals

Ron's stories were persuasive enough that his team, while still reluctant, agreed to move forward with launching a Six Sigma business improvement campaign. He recommended that team members, along with some of their key reports, should spend at least two days in an offsite workshop, learning more about the Six Sigma methodology and taking a hard look at their business to select their most significant improvement opportunities. Ron brought in an experienced Six Sigma executive coach to help the team through a leadership jumpstart workshop.

The Apex Business Group Leadership Jumpstart

The team spent a few hours learning about the New Six Sigma and hearing some of the same stories that Ron had heard about how similar businesses had turned themselves around using this methodology. By 9:30, they began to name potential projects that could benefit from Six Sigma tools. At this point, the executive coach reminded them of the first Six Sigma leadership principle—Alignment. To ensure the success of a Six Sigma business improvement campaign, the leadership team must step back from drilling directly into projects and instead make sure they are in agreement and clear on the winning strategy for their business. With no shortage of improvement project opportunities in this business, teams must only launch the projects that are most likely to improve Apex's chances of winning this year and then sustaining that winning edge for years to come. The team agreed to spend some time working on a winning strategy, which meant clarifying which customers Apex was trying to serve and what those customers were expecting from Apex. At the same time, team members needed to understand the expectations of other key stakeholders, like investors and employees. Once the team agreed on the expectations of Apex's customers and other key stakeholders, it would be in a position to articulate its mission, analyze its current environment, prioritize its strategic objectives, agree on some critical metrics, and finally begin the analysis of Apex's critical performance drivers and key processes for delivering on expectations. Team members now understood that all these activities would help them develop a shared understanding of their winning strategy and provide an integrating framework for identifying the higher-impact improvement projects. The task seemed daunting, but they were energized thinking about the possibilities.

Understanding the Voice of the Customer

The executive coach introduced the team to its first activity, designed to bring team members to a shared understanding regarding the expectations of their most important customers.

At first team members were surprised to find how disparate their views were regarding what was truly important to their customers. Many had not had direct contact with customers and found it difficult to relate expectation in real customer terms. They found that technical specifications and generic terms like "low-cost, reliable product" didn't capture their customers' true feelings. The team had been making many assumptions about what customers wanted that hadn't been validated with the actual customers. The exercise, outlined in Table 2.4, ultimately led team members to a prioritized set of statements that they believed accurately reflected customers' expectations.

Team members agreed that as a follow up to this activity they would test and validate these expectations with their customers and convert the expectations into measurable requirements. They also agreed that they would broadly communicate these prioritized customer statements across the organization to ensure that all Apex employees would be guided in their thinking and actions by the Voice of the Customer (VOC).

Table 2.4　*The Apex Business Group Voice of the*
Customer Exercise

"In Order to Meet My Expectations, You Must Provide..."
The right technology at the right time for production application
Leading, enabling technologies for research applications
Reliable products
All deliverables on time with no surprises
Global, high-quality customer support
Industry leadership in cost of ownership

Developing the Mission Statement

The voice of the customer discussion also helped the team reflect on Apex's true mission—serving key customers by providing a set of products and services essential to those customers' success. Apex's ability to secure and sustain those customers would result from the company's ability to maintain a lead over competitors. The group then developed the specifics of those insights into a draft mission statement (Table 2.5).

Team members commented that the mission statement would be useful for keeping them focused on key activities and also for helping communicate a consistent message to employees.

Getting to Alignment on Strategic Objectives

The team was now prepared to take a critical look at the Apex business. They wanted to ensure that Apex's broad business objectives stayed in alignment with stakeholder expectations and that these objectives

Table 2.5   *The Apex Business Group's Mission Statement*

"Who Do We Serve?"
Customers in wireless, data storage, and semiconductor businesses
"What Services Do We Provide?"
Leading-edge/state-of-the-art, enabling Micro technology, combined with responsive global customer support
"What Is Our Unique Competitive Advantage?"
Proprietary source technology
In-depth application knowledge
Material expertise
Installed base of loyal customers
Breadth of leading-edge technology
Flexibility and cooperativeness in tailoring R&D solutions
A core of good, talented people

would truly help the company win in the market the team had described.

Team members began by seeking to identify documents that articulated Apex's strategic objectives. The first insight came when various team members specified six different documents, ranging from a presentation for the investment community to department-level goal sheets. They wondered aloud how employees could determine the best means of helping Apex when they were receiving multiple messages about Apex's objectives.

Fortunately, the documents had common theme, and the team agreed on Apex's top strategic objectives (Table 2.6).

Table 2.6   *The Apex Business Group's Strategic Objections*

"What Are the Key Business Objectives Your Organization Must Achieve in the Next 3–5 Years?"	
Number	**Objectives**
1	• Become market-share leader in Micro device Alpha • Maintain market-share leader position in components for Micro device Beta applications
2	• Secure alliance on advanced silicon chip
3	• Establish responsive product development process
4	• Achieve effective and complete integration, particularly with sales and service
5	• Improve business systems
6	• Attract, retain, and develop key employees

Going forward, the team agreed it would work from this common set of objectives, and department-level goals and individual goals would all flow from these objectives

Analyzing the Environment

Having reached consensus on customer expectations, mission, and key objectives, the team began to wonder if Apex could meet these expectations and achieve its objectives. The executive coach suggested that a quick scan of Apex's business environment might help the team build a common understanding of the company's current state and achieve consensus on areas needing improvement.

A situation analysis followed; the ensuing discussion and the resulting summary helped team members understand just how much things had changed in just the past 12 months (Table 2.7). In an environment characterized by rapid change in customer, competitor, and landscape, Apex was busy maintaining its internal status quo.

The team agreed that the situation analysis helped build the case for change within Apex, and that those changes needed to occur soon.

Analyzing Strengths, Weaknesses, Opportunities, and Threats

The executive coach suggested that a Strengths, Weaknesses, Opportunities, and Threats (SWOT) analysis would complete the picture of the current situation and potentially yield additional insight. The activity generated a discussion and summary chart (Table 2.8) that allowed the team to recognize Apex's extreme vulnerability to the emerging competition. At the same time, team members felt renewed hope that rapid action could allow Apex to regain and sustain a winning position.

The scan of the current situation caused team members to wonder how things had slipped so dramatically during the past 12 months. How could Apex have gone from 20 percent growth and 30 percent Profit Before Tax (PBT) to negative growth and falling margins in such a short time? Hadn't they all been working 80-

Table 2.7   *The Apex Business Group's Situation Analysis*

"What Is Happening in Your Environment?"	
Customer	**Internal**
• Emerging applications • Increasingly demanding business environment • Excess capacity • Lack of venture funding • Low visibility • Reduced cap on budgets • Exclusive focus on technology buys	• Reduced visibility • Merger integration • Multiple development programs • Balancing resources with corporate initiatives • Improvement of process and documentation • Changes in sales and service • Process integration center • Strategic alliances regarding advanced silicon chip
Suppliers	**Competitors**
• Excess capacity • Increased cooperation • Shorter lead times	• Losing market share • New entrants • Dumping inventory and cutting price • Focus on components markets

hour weeks to restore revenues and recover margins? Didn't they have a performance-based culture where employees were held accountable for achieving specific goals, and weren't measurement systems in place to ensure that the company was progressing toward its goals?

Developing the Dashboard

At this point the executive coach introduced the team to the concept of a "dashboard." The coach explained that

Table 2.8   *The Apex Business Group's SWOT Analysis*

Strengths	Weaknesses
• Engineering expertise • Materials expertise • Diverse product line • Profitability • Innovation • Customer-centric policies • Accessibility	• Inconsistent product development processes • Incomplete process documentation • Weak Asian market penetration • Bit of cowboy label remains (brand)
Opportunities	Threats
• Expand into new markets • Establish quality systems player reputation • Leverage parent-company field operations • Improve operations	• Depressed market • Competitors will come after us as new • Margin erosion • Merger or acquisition by major competitors • Integration with parent company • Internal focus vs. customer focus • Employee retention

many organizations struggle to determine measures that drive accountability and behavior that improves business results. Organizations tend to fall into two problem areas. Either they narrowly focus on a single measure like revenue or profit, which causes them to lose sight of the activities that actually drive those outcomes, or they measure and track every possible activity, which creates confusion about which outcome the specific activity was supposed to impact. The solution is to get leadership alignment on a small set of measurements that are most likely to aid the leaders in monitoring progress toward their goals, while causing the organization to simultaneously balance their efforts across four dimensions: improving internal processes, achieving financial results, growing their customer base, and building employee capability. The team engaged in a process and discussions that surfaced key metrics and then reached consensus on both the metrics and stretch goals for each of the metrics. The resulting dashboard helped team members communicate the critical performance metrics and monitor progress toward the goal within each metric (Table 2.9).

The dashboard created a comprehensive picture for the team of what numerical goals Apex would have to achieve to successfully fulfill its key customer expectations and achieve its objectives. An examination of the dashboard triggered the obvious question—"How are we going to do that?" Hoping to relieve some of stress and move the team to a solution, the executive coach suggested that the team embark on a set of activities designed to answer this question. He then introduced the concept of performance driver analysis.

Surfacing the Performance Drivers

The executive coach described a performance driver as any process, system, or activity that causes a metric to increase or decrease. In its discussion of performance drivers, the Apex team learned that many different activities or processes could impact each key metric. In fact, the team faced a dilemma—for every measurement category, at least 25 performance drivers surfaced. Previously, the team would have assigned an individual to every one of the more than 100 possible performance drivers, with instructions to examine the driver and come back with a recommendation for

Table 2.9 *The Apex Business Group's Organizational Dashboard*

Key Metric ("What to Measure?")	
Internal Business	**Customer and Market**
• No-charge shipments • Reliability	• Number-one market share in all three businesses • Customer satisfaction
Financial	**Learning and Growth**
• Revenue • Cash flow • Gross margin	• Employee turnover
Stretch Goal ("How Much?")	
Internal Business	**Customer and Market**
• 20 percent reduction in warranty costs • Improve first-time yield rates by 30 percent	• 50 percent increase in market share of Total Available Market (TAM) • Strategic roadmaps with number 5 accounts
Financial	**Learning and Growth**
• 25 percent CAGR Compound annual growth rate from 2001–2004 • 50 percent gross margin • 20 percent Earnings Before Interest and Taxes (EBIT)	• Zero negative turnover

improving its the impact. Instead, the coach reminded the team of a key principle of the New Six Sigma—using the leadership team to focus the organization. The application of that principle in this case meant that the team would have to analyze and prioritize its inventory of performance drivers to determine the small set of drivers that were most likely to have the greatest impact on the metrics. The resulting analysis yielded a prioritized set of performance drivers for each metric category (Table 2.10).

Table 2.10 *The Apex Business Group's List of Performance Drivers*

Performance Drivers	
"What Factors Cause the Metric to Increase or Decrease?"	
Internal	**Customer and Market**
• Product testing • Lack of process stability • Documentation	• Product performance • Product portfolio • Sales force/integration effectiveness • Reliability, service support, responsiveness
Financial	**Learning and Growth**
• New product revenue • Increase turn rate • Value engineering • Optimized procurement	• Advancement opportunity • Communication

The analysis and prioritization process helped "clear the fog" for this leadership team and helped it determine which actions to sponsor for driving rapid improvement. Team members began to see that a focused set of improvement projects targeted toward these key drivers could indeed put them in the fast lane on the road to improvement. They were now anxious to get started; they felt that it was about time they addressed key problems that had plagued them for the past year. But they also reminded each other that people had been assigned to most of these drivers at one point or another during the past year, and these individuals had trouble making progress. That comment prompted the coach to point out how the Six Sigma approach would increase their chances of breakthrough improvement even in those areas where they had tried and failed in the past. A key difference in the Six Sigma methodology is that, after prioritizing a focused set of improvement opportunities, the leadership team must mobilize teams with clear charters established by the leadership. To determine the nature of the team that would be assigned to each driver, as well as some of the specific deliverables that would be expected from these teams, the leadership team engaged in a second level of analysis of the performance drivers to help clarify what they expected to improve relative to each driver (Table 2.11).

The group members agreed that the analysis helped validate their selection of performance drivers, and they began to see how a focused team activity could drive rapid improvement relative to each driver. They now felt prepared to write team charters and nominate team members and team leaders.

Chartering the Teams

The Apex leadership team found the process of writing team charters more difficult than they expected. As managers, team members had been launching team projects by providing teams with very broad targets,

Table 2.11 *The Apex Business Group's Performance Driver Analysis*

Performance Driver	"What Needs to Improve?"
Product/process documentation	• Implement automated business systems • Launch and implement MRP
New product revenue	• Implement new product launch process for Micro B • Launch Micro C product • Reduce product material costs/labor costs • Use consistent process to rationalize all three projects • Optimize procurement • Implement design for manufacturability
Portfolio	• Maintain focus and continued development and support of all three Micro businesses • Create communications and budgeting process to support all three • Complete sales training; tie into automated sales force and customer data base. • Locally implement S&S automated programs

Communications	• Hold quarterly leadership meetings with staff
	• Implement employee dialog process
	• Invest in key people, especially engineering:
	  • Training
	  • Career path
	• Implement and communicate business review process
	• Quarterly review of leadership talent supply

expecting that broad assignments would allow the teams flexibility and creativity in pursuit of the goals. In reality, these broad assignments left the teams confused and frustrated, because each team member had a different interpretation of "what the boss wanted."

In this case, the New Six Sigma approach suggested that, to be successful, teams must be given clear targets, a specific set of deliverables, and reasonable but challenging timelines. Excited about the potential for breakthrough improvement, the team worked diligently toward creating its team charters. Through this charter development activity, the Apex leadership team members discovered how differently each of them initially saw each project. Left to their own devices, each member would have provided different direction and communicated different expectations to various team members, a formula for team frustration and confusion. Instead, members carefully worked through objectives, deliverables, metrics, and timelines for each team. By the time the chartering process concluded, the Apex leadership team felt confident that, not only had they identified the highest impact improvement opportunities, but they also now had the right team resources positioned to execute on those opportunities. See Figure 2.1

Launching the Campaign

The Apex Business Group leaders felt like a team on a mission. They had successfully worked through their differences and now established a collective vision for Apex, a winning strategy, and clear agreement on their path to rapid business improvement. As the team prepared to launch the Apex Business Group Six Sigma business improvement campaign, its executive coach

Loan & Lease Project Charter

Business Case	Opportunity Statement
◆ This project supports the corporate goal of becoming the number 2 global financial services company by increasing customer retention and satisfaction.	◆ An opportunity to reduce customer defection (27% of the applicants) and reduce costs may be achieved by improving our loan and lease processes. The loan and lease processes currently have an average cylce time of 9.2 days, which is worse than our customer requirement of 8 days; and our application processing cost exceeds the application fee by 18%. Customer defections represent a revenue loss of $2,500,000 per year and a cost of $165,000 for partial application processing. Current Sigma is 1.6.

Goal Statement	Project Scope
◆ Reduce average loan and lease cycle time to 6 days by Oct. 1. ◆ Improve Sigma to 3.0 by Oct. 1. ◆ Reduce processing cost by 20% by the end of the year.	◆ Loan and lease processes begin with a call from the customer and end with the acceptance or rejection letter sent to the customer.

Project Plan			Team Selection	
◆ Activity	Start	End	◆ Team Characteristics/Composition	
Define	5/1	5/15	Albert Anderson	Champion
Measure	5/10	6/10	Carrie Carson	Master Black Belt
Analyze	6/5	6/20	Barry Bethel	Black Belt
Improve	7/15	8/15	Denise Davidson	Customer Service
Control	8/15	9/15	Eric Edwards	Sales Representative
Track Benefits 10/15			Frank Fischer	Loan Department

Figure 2.1   *Sample Team Charter*

helped it determine that a successful Six Sigma business improvement campaign should include some key elements:

Acceleration

Leaders identified as project sponsors would receive two days of "Champions" training that would help them effectively coach their project team in the Define, Measure, Analyze, Improve, Control (DMAIC) Six Sigma framework. The team members would receive "Green Belt" training, enabling them to assist team leaders in the application of powerful statistical analysis tools through each step of the DMAIC process. Most importantly, the team leaders would invest 20 days of their time over the next four months to learn and practice the Black Belt analytical tools designed to help them conduct thorough data gathering, analysis, design, and experimentation in every step of the project. In parallel with this training, the team members would be moving through the milestones of their project plan, guided by an expert coach who would help them apply the appropriate tools and offer best practice examples as ideas to improve their work. With coaches providing application support, instructors supplying just-in-time learning, and the Champions conducting weekly project coaching, the Apex Business Group felt confident that these teams would achieve their breakthrough improvement goals.

Governance

With the Acceleration strategy in place, the leadership team members formulated a Governance strategy. As they learned from their executive coach, an explicit Governance strategy was essential to the success of the team because it ensured that the leadership team would continue as active sponsors of the campaign. As a part of the campaign, they agreed on a schedule of monthly review sessions for the sponsors of the projects and weekly coaching sessions for each Black Belt candidate with the Champions assigned to each project. This organized review structure would ensure that the teams were making appropriate progress, getting the resources and support they needed, and—most importantly—remained on track to achieve the desired business results. As a final but crucial piece of the

Apex Business Unit Scorecard

STRATEGIC DIRECTION		PERFORMANCE MEASUREMENT	
Strategies & Objectives	Current-Year Initiatives	Key Projects	Business Results
Vision : We serve customers in Optical/Wireless, Research, Data Storage and Semi-Conductor by leading edge/state of the art enabling epitaxy technology combined with responsive global customer support. Our unique advantages include proprietary source technology, in-depth application knowledge, material expertise, installed base, breadth of MBE technology, flexible and cooperative in tailoring R&D solutions and a few good people	• Secure alliance on GaAs on Silicon • Build PIC* • Strategic roadmap with top 5 customers • Improve business systems* • Integration of sales and service, and admin • Develop and launch MOVPE • Quarterly employee meetings • GEN20 • Gas source GEN200	• Initiate and implement PLC process to rationalize 5 product projects • Launch & implement MRD, PDM, ECO • Locally implement global sales & service automated programs • Initiate quarterly talent supply mgt process • Implement business review process for employees • Optimize procurement DFM/DFA • Communications planning and budgeting process to support all 3 businesses	**Customer and Markets** •#1 market share in all 3 markets (+50% market share of TAM) •Customer satisfaction (Strategic roadmaps with #5 accounts Develop quant scorecard) **Financial** •Revenue (25% CAGR 2001-2004) •Gross Margin (50% gross margin) •Cash flow (20% EBIT) **Internal Business** •No charge shipments (20% reduction in warranty costs) •Reliability (Reduce level 3, 4, 5 incident by ___ %) **Learning and Growth** •Employee turnover (Zero negative turnover)
Strategic Objectives • Become market leader in HVM • Maintain market leader in sources and LVM • Secure alliance on GaAs on Silicon • Establish PIC • Complete and effective integration • Improve business systems • Attract, retain and develop key employees			

*Growth Opportunity

Figure 2.2   *The Apex Business Group Scorecard*

Governance strategy, the leadership team agreed on a communication strategy for the Apex Six Sigma business improvement campaign. A process of using each level of the management team to communicate the Apex vision, mission, strategic objectives, and expected business results, as well as the initiatives and project teams that would enable them to achieve these results, provided the centerpiece of the communication plan. The Apex scorecard (Figure 2.2) served as the recommended vehicle for facilitating each level of manager–employee dialog

The Apex Business Group scorecard served as a one-page articulation of the Apex winning strategy and reflected everything the leadership team had agreed upon. Wide-scale distribution of the scorecard would facilitate manager and employee dialogs relating each employee's specific quarterly goals to the Apex strategy. The scorecard also provided the context for the Apex Six Sigma business improvement campaign. The campaign's straightforward objective was to apply team resources and powerful Six Sigma tools to ensure that Apex achieves its goals fast enough to deliver breakthrough products and services for its customers and breakthrough business results for its investors. With a firm understanding of the direction established in the scorecard and the results that the Apex Six Sigma business improvement campaign would achieve, employees could once again feel excited about their future. Most importantly, the Apex leadership team felt confident that it had established a course that would lead Apex to breakthrough business results as well as sustainable improvements well into the future.

OVERVIEW OF THE NEW SIX SIGMA: ALIGN, MOBILIZE, ACCELERATE, AND GOVERN

Under the framework, training deployment begins with a process that enables the organization and the requisite leadership team to understand their current performance gaps, agree upon their improvement targets, and develop a scorecard if none exists. When a scorecard exists, the preferred approach is to derive a deployment scorecard from an existing business unit scorecard that establishes the outcome-based metrics that will guide the deployment and allow leaders to review deployment progress against their desired business results (Figure 2.3).

Align

In the case study, Alignment was realized during a four-hour session with the general managers responsible for the targeted population.

The managers received productivity analysis and benchmarking data that demonstrated the performance gap, and a facilitated activity led them to agree upon sales productivity standards and customer satisfaction goals. They then listened to analysis that demonstrated a direct link between the key drivers of both productivity and customer satisfaction and the recommended training implementation strategy. By facilitating the session with the leadership team, the training project team members successfully established results-based metrics linked directly to their sales strategy.

Insight #1: Align
Using the scorecard process as a framework, create relevant, line-of-sight improvement targets, stretch goals, and appropriate measures.

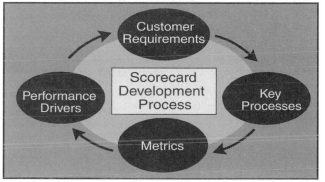

Figure 2.3   *Align*

Strong leadership support and a sustainable funding strategy resulted.

Mobilize

Having achieved leadership Alignment, the framework suggests that Mobilizing participants by deploying them in empowered teams serves as the surest path to effective implementation.

The key to mobilizing teams is to follow three principles (Figure 2.4). First, establish what the relevant team structure will be such that team members have the ability to make the necessary decisions and take the actions to operationalize the training being implemented. Once the teams are identified, their work must be recast wherever possible as customer-focused team efforts. (For example, ask what customers are we trying

Insight #2: Mobilize

Using empowered teams and a focused
project management methodology,
equip the organization to enable
people to take action.

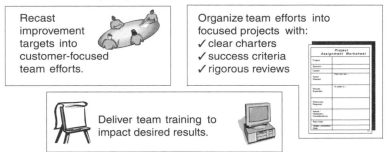

Recast improvement targets into customer-focused team efforts.

Organize team efforts into focused projects with:
✓ clear charters
✓ success criteria
✓ rigorous reviews

Deliver team training to impact desired results.

Figure 2.4 *Mobilize*

to impact and how will our training positively impact that customer.)

Second, organize team efforts into projects with clear charters, agreed-upon success criteria, and an understood management review process. The charters spell out the desired outcome and the primary activities that will lead to those outcomes in one-page documents. Success criteria establish timeframes and link the team efforts to the leadership scorecard. The leadership team communicates the process for reviewing team progress against the milestones and success criteria.

Finally, wherever possible, deliver team training on a just-in-time, as-needed basis rather than against a preset schedule. To achieve this, training must be tools-based and constructed in modules, and not necessarily dependent upon live, expert instructors. By using these principles, we enable teams to become energized, focused, and motivated to rapidly apply the training that they are receiving.

In our case study, the teams formed with a focus on specific accounts and charters, and performance goals for each account team were developed early in the process. The workshops as well as the review processes were facilitated to encourage teamwork with these account teams.

Accelerate

Once the leadership team is Aligned and the teams are Mobilized, action learning can Accelerate the overall effort, campaign planning, and clock management (Figure 2.5)

Action learning, a methodology that will be explained in the next section, ensures integration of

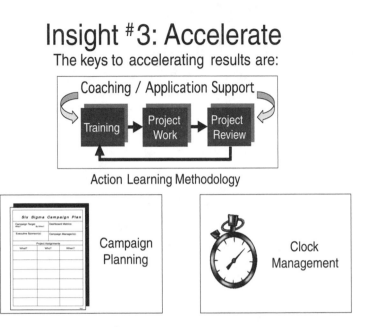

Insight #3: Accelerate

The keys to accelerating results are:

Action Learning Methodology

Campaign Planning

Clock Management

Figure 2.5 *Accelerate*

individual and project goals with training and coaching activities. Campaign planning applies basic project management principles to the implementation plan; the campaign plan details, in a project management format, the teams that have been targeted, the nature of their charters, their expected results, and the timetable under which each team is expected to complete its training and achieve its desired results. Based on an understanding that teams lose their motivation to change if their efforts fail to bear results within 60 days of the launch of those efforts, clock management causes the campaign manager to chunk team projects into 60-day deliverables and then drive the leadership team to rigorously review the teams against those deliverables at the appropriate milestones. Accelera-

Insight #4: Govern

Leadership team roles and responsibilities focused on selecting, managing, reviewing, and driving the completion of projects include:

Figure 2.6 *Govern*

tion, therefore, is achieved through application of good project management and proactive, timely intervention of facilitators, coaches, and leaders.

Within our case study, the Acceleration principles were applied by holding the account teams to the action plans and detailed timelines developed and embedded in their account plans. Rigorous account review sessions ensured achievement of the timelines.

Govern

Governance is a key piece of the New Six Sigma because it ensures that executives own the success of the projects (Figure 2.6).

Visibly making senior leaders accountable for projects and systematically reviewing project progress using the DMAIC problem-solving framework accomplishes several key goals. First, executives get early warning signs if the project needs barriers removed or additional attention. Sometimes "quick wins"—simple improvements that are cheap and easy to reverse with little risk—can make significant enough improvement that the executive should stop the improvement project and shift the Black Belt team to a more difficult problem. Second, the executive Champion has visibility to other areas that might benefit from the exact same improvement. In this way, project savings can be multiplied by managing knowledge about effective solutions in one area that can easily be applied elsewhere.

THE MODEL APPLIED TO SIX SIGMA IMPLEMENTATION

This chapter described an approach in which training serves as a strategic lever for accelerating business results for key clients. We have described the Align-Mobilize-Accelerate-Govern framework, the action learning methodology, and the role that performance contracting plays in integrating these activities with our business partners. Although we used a sales acceleration case study, this model has been best applied in the implementation of the Six Sigma quality management methodology to transform businesses and dramatically improve business results. The story is important because when Motorola introduced the Six Sigma quality management methodology in the late 1980s, the implementation strategy served primarily as a wide-scale, global-training initiative. While Motorola experienced significant returns on its training investments during the first few years, after a few years it became clear that a training-focused strategy would not achieve results that were either breakthrough in nature or sustainable over time. Faced with that reality, Motorola University tapped into its experience with action learning, change acceleration, and performance contracting to develop an implementation strategy that delivers results for Motorola business units, as well as its suppliers and customers. When viewed in its entirety, the Six Sigma implementation model provides a useful example of the integration of action learning, change acceleration, and performance contracting to achieve sustainable, breakthrough, business results.

Six Sigma Implementation—Phase One

A key tenet of a Six Sigma business improvement campaign is achieving bottom-line business results in an accelerated timeframe. Six Sigma does not measure success by hours of courseware completed but rather by achievement of results against pre-established goals in the areas of process improvement, financial gains, customer satisfaction, and innovation and growth. Establishing the goals in these categories requires an understanding of current performance levels as well as desired performance. During Phase One of the Six Sigma implementation, our activities map directly into the Alignment stage of the broad implementation framework and the preparation step of the action learning model. The performance gap analysis is completed, and the performance contract is negotiated.

Conducting a full performance excellence audit, as described earlier in this chapter, serves as the preferred approach to a performance gap analysis within the Six Sigma implementation. That audit yields data in all four results categories and generates targets of improvement opportunities. The audit itself can be performed as a wide-scale extensive audit or with a focused, cross-functional team that generates a "mini-baseline" assessment.

Upon completion of the baseline audit, the implementation moves to the leadership alignment workshop. During this two-day workshop, the business leadership team works together to develop a consensus picture of its current reality and its desired improvements.

The team learns the Six Sigma business improvement approach and then works through a series of activities that generate the following: a prioritized set of customer expectations, a Strength, Weaknesses, Opportunities, and Threats (SWOT) analysis (covered earlier in this chapter), a situation analysis, and a prioritized set of strategic objectives. While the audit results feed these activities, the team adds its perspective on the current state of the business. Having reached consensus on the current reality, the leadership team then moves to an activity that allows it to establish metrics in each of the four categories (process improvement, financial gains, customer satisfaction, and innovation and growth) and establish stretch goals in each category for the Six Sigma business improvement campaign. After establishing the goals, the leadership team works together to identify the key performance drivers within each category. Those performance drivers point directly to specific improvement opportunities, and the specific improvement opportunities become the basis for launching cross-functional teams that are chartered to achieve specific improvements within a four- to six-month timeframe. The performance goals and the team charters established during this two-day leadership alignment workshop become the basis for the performance contract with this business team. In addition to agreement regarding the performance goals and the project charters as part of the performance contract, the business unit leadership team agrees both to the resources required to support the projects (people, time, and money) and to actively engage in an ongoing project review process. This process allows it to show visible support and provide critical business guidance on a periodic basis throughout the campaign. With agreement on these critical elements, the implementation campaign moves to Phase Two—Mobilize the teams and conduct training workshops.

Six Sigma Implementation—Phase Two

With clear charters, clear outcome-based goals in hand, and enthusiastic sponsorship of their leaders, the teams are staged for success. Real success in an accelerated timeframe requires that team members receive training in processes and tools that will enable new insight and breakthrough ideas relative to solutions for these performance improvement opportunities.

The key activity during Phase Two, therefore, is the delivery of focused training workshops that build team understanding of the Six Sigma continuous improvement methodology. At the same time, individuals who play critical roles in the implementation receive focused leadership training and intensive technical training. For example, the managers, or Champions, directly responsible for the teams' results receive leadership skills training focused on empowering the team to make decisions and execute quickly and understanding the Six Sigma methodology in enough detail to provide the team with management coaching.

Team leaders, or Black Belts, receive more than 150 hours of training delivered in four week-long segments spread across four months. During these intensive technical workshops, the Black Belts learn the DMAIC methodology and the statistical tools available to add precision and deep analysis to the problem solving. Throughout this training the Black Belt candidates also develop their team leadership and project management skills. In keeping with the action learning methodology, these Black Belts work on their specific projects during these workshops and receive expert (Master Black Belt) coaching back on the job during the weeks in between the monthly workshops. This application of the action learning method allows the instructors to review project data during the workshops and allows coaches to keep the projects on track during the intervening weeks. As a result, the Black Belt candidates develop quickly and the projects deliver their results, on time, as promised.

The final target population for training is the team members (called Green Belts). Green Belt team members learn the problem-solving model, the key tools to support the model, and the roles and responsibilities of a team member in a project-team environment. The goal of the Green Belt training is to provide them with the skills they need to support their team leader in delivering the results of the project to which they have been assigned.

Six Sigma Implementation—Phase Three

Phase Three of the Six Sigma implementation parallels the structured on-the-job activities step in the action learning model. As we mentioned earlier, a key on-the-job activity in Six Sigma implementation is the expert coaching Black Belts and teams receive at set intervals across the life of their projects. The systematic, rigorous review of the projects built into the performance contract and implementation plan serves as the most important activity in this stage.

There are two levels of review for the projects. Champions (operational managers closest to the projects) receive weekly feedback from the Black Belts on the projects' progress, and the projects do not move to the next stage of completion until the Champion has signed off on the project review. A more strategic review of the project occurs on a monthly basis. During these formal reviews, the Black Belts present their projects to the Champions and to a senior leader steering committee. The Black Belts demonstrate their progress on their commitments, test potential solutions with senior leaders, and make their case for additional resources or changes in project scope where necessary. Through these review processes the teams and the projects stay tightly linked to the desired business results, and leaders stay actively engaged in the process. The ensuing tightly managed business improvement campaign achieves the predicted business results in the timeframe expected.

Ongoing Monitoring of Results

The final element of the Six Sigma implementation establishes an ongoing process of monitoring the performance of the business process where the solution was implemented to ensure that the solution delivers its promised performance improvements on a sustainable basis. Black Belt candidates become recognized as skilled Black Belts only after a financial analyst accumulates and audits these performance data.

SUMMARY

The Six Sigma business improvement campaign delivers desired business results in accelerated timeframes because the implementation plan integrates the Align-Mobilize-Accelerate-Govern framework with a full action learning methodology, enabled by a clearly articulated gap analysis and performance contract. Successful corporations like Motorola, GE, and AlliedSignal have reported millions of dollars in annual savings and demonstrated that training and development can play a strategic role in the outcome of a corporation when tightly focused on realizing the corporation's business goals.

CONCLUSION

The   Align-Mobilize-Accelerate-Govern   framework, when combined with the action learning methodology, provides a practical approach to delivering strategic business results through integrated learning solutions. The case studies demonstrate that corporate universities can use the approach to deliver bottom-line results in areas like sales effectiveness and Six Sigma business improvement. The documented success should challenge us to refine and improve the approach through wider and more consistent application. Corporate university leaders should insist on a partnership with business units that enables the type of collaboration necessary to achieve the strategic leverage illustrated in the case studies. Business unit funding of learning solutions should be viewed as investments, and the corporate university should be held accountable for the promised return on those investments. This chapter outlined an approach that makes the promise of strategic leverage a practical reality; the corporate university serves as a strategic lever to the organization when this approach is applied.

Chapter 3

Six Sigma— The Future: Reduced Risks and Improved Returns

The previous chapter showed how Motorola took Six Sigma beyond its origins as a technique for improving quality and reducing costs of poor quality. The experience gained through working with other Six Sigma practitioners such as General Electric allowed Motorola to consider the bigger picture through the use of balanced scorecards. Six Sigma is not just for quality anymore. The Six Sigma model that includes Alignment around scorecards, Mobilized Six Sigma teams, and Accelerated results within a Governance framework serves as a powerful technique for executing strategy. Strategy execution has shifted Six Sigma's focus away from simply reducing defects toward reducing variation around business goal accomplishment.

While Six Sigma is currently recognized as a powerful technique, we believe it has even greater future potential. Motorola recently started applying Six Sigma to more important and complex business problems than traditional manufacturing or service improvements. In this chapter, we begin by sharing an innovation that is just starting to pay off at Motorola—the power of our Leadership Supply process. Next, we'll share how we're evolving the next generation of Six Sigma toward shareholder value. Most significantly, we believe Six Sigma provides several important clues for improving trust of Wall Street's financial figures—so important in the post–Enron, Global Crossing, and WorldCom era.

THE NEAR FUTURE—SIX SIGMA AND LEADERSHIP SUPPLY

by Alejandro Reyes and Carey Dassatti

Two years ago, Motorola forecasted severe shortages in the number of leaders needed to both backfill positions opening up due to retirements and support anticipated growth. Aware of the growing complexity of our competitive landscape, we faced the daunting task of finding the right people to lead in this challenging environment. Motorola proactively addressed this situation through Leadership Supply, an entirely new and integrated process for managing senior executives. To create this program properly, we followed the principles of Define, Measure, Analyze, Improve, and Control (DMAIC)—the cornerstone of Six Sigma.

Defining the Gap—The Demand Problem

First, we reviewed data on the future environment Motorola would face when sourcing new leaders. A variety of government sources suggest that, by 2010, the global pool of business leaders between the ages of 35 and 45 will decrease by 15 percent. At the same time, economic growth projections indicate that corporate demand for those future leaders will increase by more than 25 percent. These statistics show that companies must focus on their leadership pipelines now to ensure that they attract and retain a disproportionate share of this talent pool in the future.

Motorola hired Bain & Company to test this finding, and Bain's study estimated that the average corporation already faced a 25 percent shortage of employees who show the potential to develop into executives. Bain concluded that such a leadership shortfall could cost a business as much as a 10 percent return on the cost of capital employed.

Further, 75 percent of 13,000 executives surveyed by McKinsey & Co. indicated that they are chronically short of leadership talent. The same study found that companies that did a better job of attracting, developing, and retaining highly talented managers earned 22 percentage points higher return to shareholders.

In this context, Motorola launched its project to assess and project demand for leaders. First, we compared the number of leaders required to run Motorola with the numbers of leaders expected to retire, be recruited away, and leave voluntarily, as well as the volume who would fail to perform and leave involuntarily. At the same time, we added the speed of development of the next-generation leaders to the supply side of our estimates. Our forecasts suggested that in 2004 Motorola would face a shortfall of approximately 200 general managers or leaders of critical functions.

Measuring and Analyzing the Gap

Next, we studied Motorola's existing processes for managing leaders and contrasted them with the leadership supply processes used by other successful firms. An important aspect of the diagnosis was how we framed the problem. We decided to think about the problem in the same manner as an order-to-cash process—we followed leaders' careers from before they joined Motorola until they exited, just as an order-to-cash process follows from the time customers place an order until payment is received. This holistic, lifecycle approach to defining the processes allowed us to identify leadership supply subsystems to measure and analyze individually in an integrated end-to-end leadership supply process. Key interrelated subprocesses include the following:

- External recruitment and selection
- Training
- Career planning and development
- Performance management
- Compensation and benefits
- Succession planning/talent management

- Retention
- Internal selection/placement and promotion
- Outplacement

Bain helped us complete our diagnosis, including external benchmarking, and weave together best-practice leadership processes. We directed Bain to select the benchmarking companies very carefully, with a preference for companies that consistently create unique shareholder value rather than those known for great leadership development. It was important to focus this initiative on producing business results, not just on solving the leadership gap.

We identified several critical elements consistently present in the sample of world-class leadership supply processes we studied:

- Leadership and performance criteria specific to the position drove the performance evaluation and management process.
- An objective, balanced performance evaluation and management process is the cornerstone of the entire leadership supply system.
- Performance management data provide a rigorous, ongoing fact base to support differential investments in top performers.
- Leaders manage their human talent as aggressively as they do their P&Ls.
- Talent is managed as a portfolio and segmented by performance, behaviors and potential.
- Top companies consider talent a corporate-wide resource, not one to be hoarded/managed by individual business units.

In addition to our benchmarking exercise, we looked inside Motorola for lessons about current processes that worked well and those that didn't. Eighty representatives of Motorola's global businesses contributed interviews, processes, and tools that we analyzed to assess current capabilities. In the end, we incorporated the best practices we uncovered into Leadership Supply, an end-to-end process redesign (Figure 3.1).

The establishment of a corporate-wide definition of leadership served as one of Leadership Supply's earliest successes. Previously, judging leadership capability had been confusing—there were as many definitions of the term as managers in the world. We clearly needed a

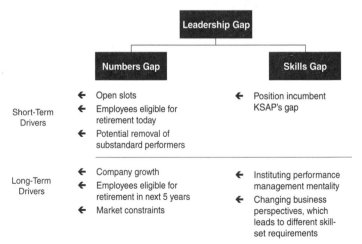

Components of the Gap

Compounding the external constraint on leadership talent were gaps between Motorola's internal needs and resources.

Leadership Gap

	Numbers Gap	**Skills Gap**
Short-Term Drivers	← Open slots ← Employees eligible for retirement today ← Potential removal of substandard performers	← Position incumbent KSAP's gap
Long-Term Drivers	← Company growth ← Employees eligible for retirement in next 5 years ← Market constraints	← Instituting performance management mentality ← Changing business perspectives, which leads to different skill-set requirements

Figure 3.1 *The Motorola Leadership Supply Gap*

common language to get started. Based on General Electric's leadership values, the Motorola Office of Leadership, led by Sandy Ogg, introduced the "4e's + Always 1 Leadership" standards:

- **eNVISION**—Generates the vision, strategies, and viable plans to achieve it. Identifies meaningful and innovative change that produces profitable growth.
- **eNERGIZE**—Excites employees, customers, and partners around winning ideas. Brings extraordinarily high personal energy to all work. Creates an environment where team members find opportunities to contribute and feel the passion to excel.
- **eDGE**—Cuts to the essence of what is important. Makes bold, timely decisions. Insists that the organization must outperform expectations. Brings a healthy dissatisfaction with the way things are. Makes tough calls when the business or individuals fail to perform.
- **eXECUTE**—Achieves significantly better and faster results than competitors by employing innovative, proven, and rigorous management practices. Personally meets commitments and keeps promises.
- **eTHICS**—Conducts business ethically always and everywhere. Treats all people and all cultures with respect and dignity. Keeps personal ambitions and emotional reactions from interfering.

Our leadership standards provide a common language for explaining what is considered a great leader at Motorola. We describe our leadership standards in terms of 17 observable behaviors. These standards help us move Motorola through the cultural transformations needed to survive and win in the marketplace today and in the future.

Implement and Institutionalize

Based on the data gathered in the diagnostic phase of the project, we launched a global process redesign effort. We formed 10 redesign teams with seven to eight people on each team, including line executives and Human Resources experts, and we knew that to ensure the effectiveness of the final process, it was important that this redesign effort involve the people who were ultimately going to have to use the system. Ogg gave the teams 120 days to redesign their subprocess; additionally, he assigned one "master" team the task of integrating the systems and providing support to all the processes. It soon became clear that the subprocesses could be simplified into the following six interdependent processes:

- **Performance management**—Measure results to expectations and goals, and assess behaviors against the 4 e's + Always 1 standards, calibrated relative to peers. Apply consequences to drive improved business results.
- **Talent management**—Use a systematic approach that proactively identifies, tracks, develops, and manages global and diverse critical internal talent.
- **Recruit and select**—Use processes to attract world-class external talent and skill sets to enhance business performance and drive superior results.
- **Career planning and development**—Provide tools that allow individuals to develop and improve the skill sets that drive improved business outcomes.

- **Transition assistance**—Provide alternative career opportunities, both externally and internally, for individuals whose skill sets are misaligned with the requirements of their positions.
- **Rewards**—Link executive rewards and benefit administration to support and reinforce the Leadership Supply process such that it enables differential investment decisions.

The redesign teams came back with initial implementation recommendations in each of these areas, as well as detailed process maps.

Leadership Supply Web

Motorola's Web-based system for talent management is the engine behind the Leadership Supply processes. It is a repository for experience, performance, and career information on Motorola leaders, as well as a collection of applications central to the process including the following modules:

- **Online talent profiles**—Essentially a structured online resume, the talent profile is a shared space on the Talent Web where Motorola and the individual leader can record and display capabilities that can be applied to various roles. In addition to factual information about the executive's past, it also contains facts about the current role and future aspirations.
- **Online leadership assessments**—Motorola uses Web-enabled assessments to measure each individual leader against the 4e's + Always 1 Leadership standards.

- **Online calibration of ratings and rankings—** The collective identification of the most- and least-effective leadership talent, the calibration is used for summarizing the facts on a group of leaders and then ranking them relative to one another. The data sources include leadership assessments, how well the leaders accomplished their goals from the performance management system, and other considerations like job scope, complexity, difficulty of goals, time in position, and breadth of experience.

- **Online position profiles—**Position profiles are developed for all job families within Motorola. Each profile summarizes the knowledge, experience, and skill requirements for a particular position; it also includes the market value of this position and a one-page summary, with the ability to provide details when needed. We call positions critical to Motorola's business success "most leveraged positions."

In addition to these "high-tech" applications, the Leadership Supply process features a number of "high-touch" processes:

- Quarterly performance-management feedback and career-planning dialogues with each executive

- Semi-annual talent management meetings where individuals and organizations are discussed, and moves planned

- Annual calibration meetings at all levels to ensure fair and consistent ratings and rankings of individuals

- General management training outsourced to Kellogg Graduate School of Management at Northwestern University
- Personalized recruitment and assimilation of key talent from outside and inside Motorola

The Office of Leadership

Several teams emphasized that new Leadership Supply process, as a critical business issue, would not succeed without dedicated resources reporting to Motorola's CEO, Chris Galvin. In the past, each subsystem had been managed by different Human Resources organizations, but the teams felt that Galvin should now act as the "Chief Human Resources Officer for Top Talent." Galvin approved the recommendation and named Ogg, the project's lead executive, to run the Office of Leadership. Galvin further committed to spending a third of his time on this new role during the first year of operation.

Control-Sustaining Leadership Supply

Today, each Motorola business sector is required to use Leadership Supply tools and processes to identify the most effective leaders and compare this list with the list of most-leveraged positions. The resulting grid spotlights gaps between the need for top talent (most-leveraged positions) and the performance of existing talent. Further, it enables fact-based discussion about talent gaps, talent moves, diversity, and career progression. A key benefit to our Leadership Supply process is that Motorola can very quickly replace critical positions left open by unexpected moves.

Six Sigma and Leadership Development

Embedding Six Sigma techniques into systematic leadership development programs serves as an important part of the Leadership Supply process. Like our colleagues at GE, we believe that by making the Six Sigma business improvement model a teachable experience we are building a fast, money-making leadership-development engine—by creating leaders with Green Belts and Black Belts, we are creating an adaptive, evolving organization that creates its own future.

At Motorola, the synchronization of process steps throughout the Leadership Supply process and particularly in the performance management, rewards, and compensation systems ensures that the right assignments are given to the right people. In particular, we carefully make sure to formally assign the most important business problems to the most talented individuals. Next, we give the high-potential leaders great support structures to increase their probability of success—sponsors, mentors, Six Sigma Champions, and Black Belts support leaders in getting their Green Belts while solving a business problem.

In addition, we have our senior executives coach for these managers. Motorola views these efforts as solving many problems with one great program: Six Sigma. We're increasing our chances of solving important business problems and, at the same time, we're differentially investing in the skills of our high-potential leaders, a great strategy for showing top leaders that we value them and don't want to loose them.

Accomplishments

The Motorola Office of Leadership has been operating since February 2000. The most relevant outcomes can be classified in these categories:

- **Organizational strength**—63 new leaders in the 100 most important jobs during 2001 and 2002, covering 75% of those positions with internal talent.
- **Leadership renewal**—Talent in critical positions: The COO and CFO were renewed in first 100 days of 2002—one of those within hours. In addition, the total number of officers was reduced 25% in 2002.
- **Retention of critical talent**—Retained 98% of our most effective executives during 2001 and 2002.
- **The new Leadership Supply system, institutionalized**—An objective and rigorous ranking of all senior executives is established in Motorola and recognized as reliable data source for performance management and talent management purposes.

THE DISTANT FUTURE OF SIX SIGMA

by Matt Barney

Leadership Supply is just the beginning of where we're taking Six Sigma. By incorporating ideas from Finance, Operations Research, Computer Science, and Organizational Psychology, we're creating the near and distant future of Six Sigma. We believe Six Sigma's future includes broad areas of application that haven't yet been fully explored, including diverse uses ranging from improving financial reporting and the future of

Black Belts to better innovation and successful philanthropy.

Six Sigma and Shareholder Value

In the future, Six Sigma will play a significant role in helping executives manage risk and improve shareholder returns. Just as traditional applications of Six Sigma build trust in customer relationships by ensuring that products and services consistently deliver as promised, we believe Six Sigma can also enhance trust with analysts and shareholders. Experts have identified the recent breakdown of integrity in traditional financial reporting processes, epitomized by extreme examples such as Enron and WorldCom, as a failure of the self-regulating mechanisms in both government and industry (Lev, 2002). When used correctly, we believe Six Sigma can help investors regain confidence in financial reporting.

Regaining Wall Street's Trust

High-profile collapses and financial restatements have frequently been blamed for causing serious injury to the American economy, specifically in regard to the extended economic downturn of 2002. In a report to Congress delivered February 2, 2002, Baruch Lev, a financial reporting expert, identified three root causes of the financial reporting. First, he noted that companies could cook the books because they had inappropriately close relationships with their auditors. Second, government regulators, generally slow and late to enforce audit failures through litigation, didn't publicize the instances where they succeeded in stopping wrongdoers. This contributed to a climate suggesting unethical behavior went unpunished. Third, financial reporting has been far too narrow and traditionally misses important components of shareholder value, including the value inherent in relationships with customers and suppliers, the cost of unexecuted obligations in future periods, the value of intangible assets, and the lack of comprehensive disclosure of risk exposures. We believe Six Sigma techniques and methods can improve all three of the areas identified by Lev.

In the first problem area—unethical executives who cook the books—Six Sigma methods can help by establishing Human Resources processes that select and manage the ethical behaviors of executives. Many companies successfully use integrity tests to predict good performance and ethical behaviors before hiring employees (Ones, Viswesvaran, and Schmidt, 1993). Because it's nearly impossible to detect conscientious, prudent leaders in a structured interview, companies should systematically employ these tests when selecting executives and financial professionals.

At the same time, no personnel selection process is foolproof—it is just as critical for companies to establish strong performance management processes that promote ethical behavior of managers. At Motorola, CEO Chris Galvin has consistently emphasized ethics, both in terms of role modeling expected behaviors and managing employee performance. In fact, he has led the effort to establish ethics as a regular metric in Motorola's performance appraisal system; all leaders must score high to continue their employment. The few leaders who slip through the preventive integrity test can be caught with good performance management sys-

tems before they cause much harm. Similarly, to further address the root cause of financial reporting
problems, companies must establish processes that
clearly demonstrate that audits are independent, verifi-
able, and strive toward objectivity. Six Sigma measurement methods and tools are invaluable in ensuring the
integrity of financial and other processes.

Second, government regulators can more fully over-
see truthfulness in financial reporting by establishing
Six Sigma processes in the public sector. In particular,
we strongly recommend that the Securities and
Exchange Commission (SEC) use scorecards to establish publicly tracked measures that ensure financial
information integrity. Kaplan and Norton call these
"impact maps." These should include metrics on the
success and volume of audits, errors, failures, litigation
settlements, and Black Belt projects underway to make
improvements. Today's Web-enabled data sharing technologies and standards (e.g., XML) make it easy, fast,
and cheap to provide such visibility—as long as regulators are prepared to manage regulatory and oversight
processes with Six Sigma techniques to ensure financial information integrity. For both corporations and
governments, Six Sigma is key to ensuring financial
process validity because it is based on the same underlying need for integrity that drove its genesis at Motorola. Bob and Chris Galvin's strong focus on doing the
right thing underlies why Motorola invented it—to
ensure that we consistently and honestly deliver value
to customers, which in turn produces a feeling that
we're as good as our word. Financial processes need to
strive for this same underlying value, and we believe

ensuring trustworthiness in financial data is Six Sigma's legacy.

Six Sigma has perhaps the most potential to help with the third problem area—valuing intangibles. Six Sigma experts know that there is error in all measurement, and financial measurements are no different; in Measurement Systems Analysis (MSA), a traditional Six Sigma technique to analyze and reduce measurement error, this is called reliability or precision. The accounting profession, in contrast, traditionally assumes that income statements and balance sheets are without mistakes. Even if they acknowledge error, they don't report it, asking the reader to "trust them" that any mistake is trivial.

In addition to highly publicized ethical lapses by firms like Global Crossing, Enron and WorldCom, in 2002 an unacceptably large number of companies restated their earnings. Recent events demonstrate that financial statements do include errors, and unfortunately not always in trivial amounts. This is particularly true because people—accountants and auditors—do a significant portion of the work, and human intensive processes are more difficult to optimize than machine-intensive processes. Sometimes, auditors and accountants have different opinions about how to classify certain kinds of costs.

This difference can be detected using Six Sigma methods. Two significant benefits can be gained by using Six Sigma's Measurement Systems Analysis (MSA) techniques to look at inter-auditor reliability, and systematically report on the error variability inherent in the numbers. First, firms can build higher levels of trust with their shareholders by being honest about how much or little error there is in financial figures. In the current economic environment, candidness in financial reporting can be a significant differentiator in market cap valuations. Second and perhaps more importantly, senior leaders can quantify financial errors and use Six Sigma techniques to reduce financial measurement error to trivial levels.

Measuring and Managing Tangibles and Intangibles

Six Sigma can also address Lev's concerns about firms not systematically showing the value of their intangibles on standard financial reports. In particular, the work of Jeanne DiFrancesco (2000, 2002) of ProOrbis suggests that the answer to credibly and validly measuring intangibles lies in changing how we think about valuing all assets, tangible and intangible. The ProOrbis model suggests that classic financial valuation is flawed because the true value of an asset in a going concern isn't the liquidation price or purchase price minus depreciation. If the liquidation or market price were the true value and the company couldn't use the asset at a higher benefit inside the firm, it would be better off selling it to the highest bidder. ProOrbis promotes the idea that assets are valuable when they do work helpful to the firm.

This model suggests that once the business strategy is defined, the value chain or business processes must be developed to execute the strategy. To build the processes, managers must make decisions about the right mix of assets—machinery, buildings, technology, and human performance—needed to maximize customer and shareholder value. When assembling the right configuration of physical, technological, and human assets to work for the firm, they are executing what Six Sigma calls the "voice of the business," ensuring that the mix will perform to specifications dictated by the business strategy. The strategy articulates financial goals, such as margin requirements, as well as desired market outcomes, including customer requirements. Once the strategy is complete, the senior leaders design the firm's value chain to ensure the right kind and mix of assets are present at each step in the process. When assets are specified in this way, Six Sigma can help operationally define all the performance specifications required to successfully execute the strategy. To fully manage all firm assets, performance specs should be defined simultaneously for people, machinery, and technology—because if anyone doesn't perform to levels needed, the entire system can be suboptimized. Figure 3.2 outlines the types of physical and human performance, as well as the attributes underlying the performance that must be managed by organizational subprocesses supporting the value chain.

Because these new valuation models look at the organization as one big system, or a set of interrelated processes, they all must work together to realize the desired value. At the same time, the sum of all investments in all assets must fit within the margin goals articulated by the business strategy. This approach to valuing intangibles suggests that a key to understanding the value created by tangible or intangible assets is to understand the difference between true costs—resources that get burned up in a period (e.g., travel, energy, raw materials) and investment in assets that do work over multiple periods.

Machine and Human Performance in Context

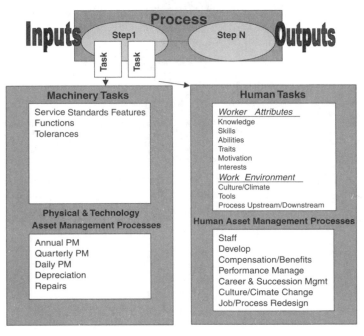

Figure 3.2 *Machine and Human Performance in Context*

Second, this approach suggests a new way to measure the value of assets. It suggests that the value of the assets—tangible or intangible—is the difference between the value of the products or services and the inputs that were burned up to create them. DiFrancesco suggests that the difference between "throughputs" and "inputs" is how all assets in the firm create value in a going concern. If a company isn't a going concern (i.e., is bankrupt), its value is the typical liquidation or market value of its assets (DiFrancesco,

2002). Further, the model suggests that you can understand the effectiveness of your assets in producing this value by using a new Return on Investment (ROI) approach:

Value of Core Assets = Throughputs – Inputs

Return on Investment = Value of Core Assets / Investments in Core Assets

A third key is to optimize the configuration of the use of each asset type in every step in the process. If you have too much capacity in one type of asset in a particular part of the process relative to the goals, you waste resources that can't possibly help create value. Importantly, this approach suggests that investments in all assets must be actively engineered together to optimally realize customer, market, and financial goals on the scorecard. It further suggests that the performance of each asset in creating value can only be understood at the organizational level—where dollars are collected and customers are delighted. All of these ideas are very well suited to Six Sigma's focus on process, and they augment Six Sigma by specifying better equations by which we can value investing in various assets and improvement projects.

This model also suggests that the biggest constraint to creating shareholder value in the company is that point where the gap between the required and actual asset performance is greatest. All assets—work done by people, machines, and buildings—have value only in the context of the overall value the firm will produce. The next two figures show the overall value chain, or process, of a firm both without a bottleneck in operations (Figure 3.3) and with a bottleneck (Figure 3.4).

Value Chain Without Bottleneck

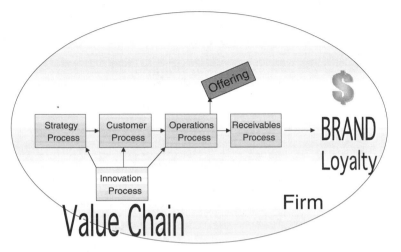

Figure 3.3 *Value Chain Without Bottleneck*

This new valuation approach shows that if you understand the work each asset class is doing, you have the ability to pinpoint the places where improvement projects will have the biggest impact. Further, financial forecasting can be improved by measuring the size of the biggest constraint in the core process.

To leverage these ideas and build on the power of classic Black Belt expertise, Six Sigma will start to borrow ideas from other statistically oriented sciences— Economics, Operations Research, Industrial-Organizational Psychology, and Management Science. In particular, a class of techniques called stochastic models (i.e., Markov chains) and operations research simulation tools can help model the real-time performance of assets in a system. In the future, the most important

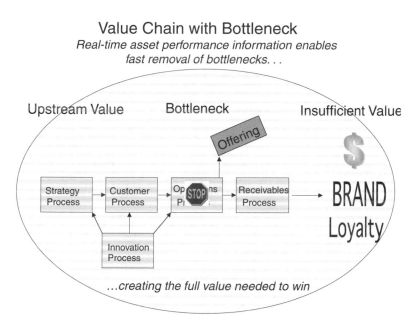

Figure 3.4 *Value Chain with Bottleneck*

organizational IT systems will combine these new intangible asset valuation techniques with stochastic models to manage financial value creation in real time. Because the New Six Sigma already connects processes and people, from the individual employee and machine through processes all the way to real-time balanced scorecards, the new valuation techniques are an extremely powerful addition.

These approaches are laborious without the invention of new software called Workflow. Workflow is a class of powerful software that manages work in processes. While many white-collar work environments today execute processes through email, without performance-tracking capability, there is significant potential as organizations become aware of Workflow to improve processes. Today, no existing workflow software includes these intangible asset valuation measures, but it's just a matter of time before they do, because it appears to be the only way to practically track value flowing through complex organizations. When you consider the new approaches to valuation together with workflow and scorecard software, it becomes apparent that balanced scorecards are just snapshots of the areas where senior executives believe serious business constraints are found. Figure 3.5 graphically depicts the relationship between workflow and balanced scorecard measurements. With these innovations, Six Sigma will allow organizations to rapidly change themselves in response to market conditions and strategy shifts.

Innovations in Project Selection

These new intangible asset valuation techniques also suggest the specific places and actions where Six Sigma Black Belt projects will have the best payoff. In classic Six Sigma applications, leaders choose projects either by intuition, return on investment, or net present value methods. Advanced work in an approach called "real options," however, uses statistical estimates of probability of various outcomes, a more useful approach for pinpointing the best projects, given that managers often have choices about projects and investments. Many times, managers can choose to invest a smaller amount in the near term and defer the decision to invest after more information is available (and consequently less risk is involved).

When using real options, Six Sigma Black Belts must relearn the truism that all variation is evil. With

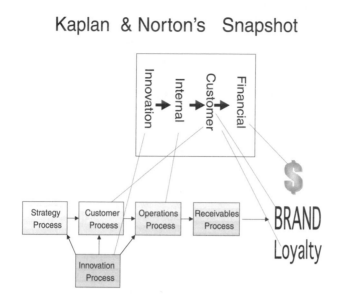

Figure 3.5 *Relationship between workflow and balanced scorecard measurements*

real options, decisions with more variability (i.e., more choices) have more value than those with less (Copeland and Antikarov, 2001). This is because choices with more variability have bigger upside potential than those with less variability. Real options, by combining the new work on valuation, with techniques such as Monte Carlo analysis and linear programming, allows executives to further mitigate risk and maximize returns. Monte Carlo looks at the probability and distribution of various outcomes, while linear programming provides precise strategies for optimizing choices about the best portfolio of projects or decisions to diversifying risk and maximizing economic value creation. By combining these techniques, leaders of Six Sigma efforts can treat their improvement projects as a portfolio of investments and consider Black Belt project diversification, risk, and return just like any other type of investment. At Motorola University, we are currently studying whether these new techniques do a better job of valuation and forecasting than classic financial models, and we are eager to integrate the findings into the future of Six Sigma.

The Future of Mitigating Risk

Several risk mitigation strategies that synchronize well with Six Sigma have already proven effective—they just aren't yet known to Six Sigma practitioners.

One of the most important contributions of Six Sigma is the focus and measurement of customer requirements. Traditional Six Sigma practitioners use a variety of largely qualitative and survey techniques to specify the particulars of the product and service desired. This typically starts with listening to the Voice of the Customer (VOC) and converting this voice into Critical Customer Requirements (CCRs) and ultimately metrics that specify factors Critical to Quality (CTQs). The problem with the current approach, particularly with Motorola's experience with software requirements, is that customer requirements seem to change faster than an organization's ability to adapt. Two new Six Sigma approaches can help assess customer require-ments more accurately and with more stability.

First, a technique called policy capturing can reverse-engineer customer decisions about features, functions, and specifications. For many years, cognitive and organizational scientists have used policy capturing to discover the underlying decision-making processes and variables that people use. Since customers are people too, companies can now use these techniques to reverse-engineer the customer's decision-making processes that created customer requirements in the first place. Customers' decision-making processes are less likely to change as fast as specific requests or specifications. By understanding models of customer decision making, Six Sigma Black Belts should better understand how and why clients have specified their current requirements and forecast future customer requirements, thereby giving advanced notice faster than the competition. We believe today's Master Black Belts can adopt this technique to more accurately assess the particular specifications and requirements of customers.

Second, lists of customer requirements are often very long, sometimes hundreds of variables long. Traditionally, Six Sigma hasn't had a good way to identify the vital few—or the underlying customer need. Multidimensional scaling, principle components, and factor analysis are powerful data-reduction techniques—but the vast majority of Black Belts have never even heard of them, let alone used them. Used correctly, they can do a great job of summarizing the customer requirements that represent the underlying customer need.

A still more-powerful technique called structural equation modeling can also improve the accuracy and stability of requirements. Structural equation modeling can be used to model a variety of business phenomena, not limited to customers. Applied to customer requirements, Master Black Belts can test specific models of customer delight relative to features, while at the same time modeling financial outcomes such as return on equity or cash flow. Unlike some statistical tools, structural equation models have the ability to test competing models where different variables affect dollars and delight. If Black Belts gain skill in these sophisticated tools, they will substantially improve their focus on the most important customer requirements as well as improve the validity and stability of improvement projects.

The last area we will discuss in mitigating risk involves simulations. Today, many Master Black Belts use process simulation tools to model processes before implementation as part of Design for Six Sigma (DFSS). This helps identify unforeseen bottlenecks and remove them to ensure that new or redesigned processes work right the first time. But few Black Belts know about project simulation tools designed to optimize a project's work breakdown structure. Research out of Stanford and Carnegie Mellon on predicting successful projects has created spin-off companies that not only help mitigate the risk of tasks failing, but also model the organizational design that could constrain approvals at key points in a project. Future Six Sigma leaders will require project simulations before starting improvement projects and process simulations before implementing improvements. Together, the risk of failure can be mitigated significantly.

The Future of Black Belts

We believe that the future of Black Belts is heavily dependent on using Six Sigma on itself. Many companies and academic research have identified optimal processes for selecting, training, and managing employees that are unknown to practitioners of Six Sigma.

In the first part of the Six Sigma development process, it's important that you select candidates for Green Belt or Black Belt who have a high aptitude for being successful. Some of these areas aren't trainable—such as the ability to learn quickly. Based on research done by the Six Sigma Business Improvement Group at Motorola University, candidates for Black Belt must have high levels of:

- Cognitive ability (intelligence)
- Integrity/conscientiousness—doing the right things right
- Extraversion and agreeableness—the interpersonal abilities of initiating and enhancing relationships

Without these talents in a Black Belt, there's no chance that they'll ever get onto the CEO's speed dial when there are big picture business improvements needed. With them, Black Belts can be extremely effective, with consistently better project outcomes. Part of the future of Black Belts will involve using these sophisticated Black Belt management techniques, so that Black Belts are treated as a precious asset that requires careful use of these screening tools to nurture.

The visionary Black Belts and quality leaders in Motorola's cellphone business (Personal Communications Sector) Greg Milano and Kevin Kent have begun implementing a systematic Black Belt development information system. The information system is a cradle-to-grave management system of all aspects of Black Belt from admission to candidacy, through development and stock option and cash rewards through mentoring

and Master Black Belt. These workflow systems auto-
mating Black Belt development are a key component to
future high-quality Black Belt programs.

Future Black Belt Skills

Today, most Master Black Belts are experts at solving
business problems in quality domains. Six Sigma's
future application will require Black Belts to learn new
techniques across a variety of disciplines. Business
needs will demand ever-higher levels of Black Belt skill
in leading and managing change, as well as improving
all parts of business processes with the right tools. This
means the profile of the Black Belt will change from
largely engineering skills to interdisciplinary expertise—with the common grounding of the scientific
method combined with an MBA.

Change Skills

Leading and managing change provides the biggest
opportunity for improvement in Black Belts. Black
Belts will need to create better burning platforms to
ensure fast, sustained improvement in a variety of disciplines. Further, Black Belts must take the study of
Industrial-Organizational Psychology much more seri-
ously than they have in the past. By understanding the
root causes of employee behavior and using validated
models, they'll be much better equipped to manage
change across areas as diverse as Law, Marketing,
Facilities, Finance, and Human Resources.

Industrial-Organizational Psychology

Black Belts will need to learn extensively from the experts at measuring and improving employee performance: Industrial-Organizational psychologists. Black Belts have a great deal to learn about the statistically derived models that can predict which job candidates have a high probability of performing well; measuring the impact of training; crafting valid measures of employee performance; and measuring and scientifically managing organizational culture change. I-O psychologists can share a host of quantitative techniques along with sophisticated technical knowledge about employee performance engineering that is critical for the success of Black Belts working in human-intensive processes. Motorola used these very techniques in the Leadership Supply process described earlier. We used the processes optimized by I-O psychologists, as well as their tools for creating assessments of leadership capability and performance, designing succession plans, forming development paths, and compensating executives. HR statistical methods will be required in future Black Belt toolkit, since work increasingly blends sophisticated machinery with even more-sophisticated humans (i.e., biologists, engineers).

The good news is that many of the quantitative skills required for analyzing HR problems but unknown to modern Black Belts are also useful in Marketing, Quality, and Engineering. Based on the same statistical, customer, and business improvement principles as the classic Black Belt knowledge base, these tools are important new areas that give extra power. Techniques that show the reliability of ratings between two or more people are important in both Market Research and

Human Resources to establish good measurement systems, for example. Similarly, to appropriately characterize market segments, Black Belts will need to learn data reduction and summary tools such as inverse principle axis factor analysis, and graphical tools to show segment groupings or customer preferences such as multidimensional scaling. To fully understand why customers or employees defect to the competition, Black Belts increasingly will use a tool called survival analysis. Lastly, new prediction and modeling tools such as hierarchical linear modeling and neural networks will play important roles in continuously improving forecasts about areas as diverse as finance, customer loyalty, and employment brand image.

Financial Acumen

Wall Street does not forgive companies who miss financial forecasts on the downside; to ensure accurate forecasts, Black Belts need to learn new techniques including time series analysis, time series-based structural equation models, and other econometric methods. Black Belts also must learn more about real options valuation. As discussed previously, combining probability estimates of decisions together with discounted cash-flow techniques provides a much more powerful method of making organizational decisions (e.g., picking improvement projects) than ever before.

Six Sigma and Innovation

Critics of Six Sigma have sometimes argued that it isn't useful for improving innovation (*American Banker*, 2002). In fact, there is a long and fruitful history of the application of statistical methods to improving people-intensive processes of all kinds, including creative research, development, and innovation.

First, many Six Sigma practitioners also have expertise in a technique from Russia called TRIZ, which stands for the "theory of inventive problem solving" (translated from Russian). It involves decomposing an engineering problem into a basic structure showing contradictions and using software to show how the problem has been solved in other domains. This technique has successfully generated a variety of creative solutions to Six Sigma engineering problems.

But there are even more useful tools and processes that the Six Sigma community hasn't known about. Traditionally, process improvements related to creativity and innovation are unknown to Six Sigma practitioners because successful applications mostly have been published in academic journals by researchers who haven't historically connected themselves to Six Sigma business improvement.

Three creativity process innovations are especially important. The first is hiring creative people. Steven Guestello of Marquette University has written about cognitive and personality variables that vary between people and predict creativity. He reports that many studies have shown that these validated tests consistently forecast which people in an organization will excel at innovating (Guestello, 1995, pp. 303–304).

Research has identified that creative people are divergent thinkers—and there are good assessments that can help companies find divergent thinkers in their hiring process. Furthermore, all creative people share a common personality profile (Table 3.1).

Table 3.1   *Common Personality Profile of Creative People*

Personality Profile of Creative People
1. Abstract thinkers
2. Introverted
3. Assertive
4. Serious
5. Nonconforming
6. Socially bold
7. Sensitive
8. Imaginative
9. Experimental and open-minded
10. Self-sufficient—prefer working alone

Of course, innovative personality traits have to be present in a person with domain-specific knowledge—a creative physician won't do a good job at innovation in software engineering. By including good measures of cognitive divergence, creative personality traits, and intrinsic motivation in addition to domain-specific skills in employee selection, organizations can systematically improve their people's ability to innovate. This is especially true for employees whose job it is to create (e.g., researchers).

Second, research suggests that matching each person's creative style with work requirements can be an important driver of innovative performance. Researchers have identified three major styles that organizations can exploit to their benefit (Sternberg and Lubart, 1991). Some people are very good at generating new ideas, while others sort out good from bad ideas, and still others translate abstract ideas into practical reality. Depending on what part of the innovation process needs improvement, organizations can select employees based on their creative style and the process-step need. For example, it would be best for researchers to favor generating totally new ideas and sorting out the good from the bad, while developers would do well to translate creativity into realization.

A third and perhaps most important part of the innovation process is the environment in which the creative employees must work. Harvard's Teresa Amabile has shown in many applied settings that cognitive abilities, traits, and styles are necessary but not sufficient to produce innovations (Amabile, 1996). In addition, her work demonstrates that the person must also have domain-relevant skills, a work style conducive to creativity, and motivation to complete tasks. Amabile finds task motivation to be the most important component in driving creativity; intrinsic or internal motivation (rather than external rewards like dollars), in particular, is the key to reaching the highest levels of creativity.

Amabile's work with real companies strongly suggests that once you've picked the right creative people, you cannot leverage their full potential unless you put them into a work environment conducive to creativity. She suggests that time and resources, positive and constructive feedback that is work or task focused, a playful and experimental climate, and a safe environment for risk taking are all necessary. Inhibitors to creative performance include supervisory surveillance as well as time pressure and stress unrelated to the creative tasks (Amabile, 1996).

A key driver of a creative work environment is the organizational climate and work style of management. The best environment includes positive emotional state, a concern for creativity, tolerance for individual differences between team members, and a willingness to take risks. The best managers of innovative employees have a personality profile similar to that of creative people—they are dominant, social, bold, and intelligent; they are less rule-oriented, more sensitive, more imaginative, and more unconventional than other managers; and they prefer to work alone rather than in groups.

Six Sigma and Philanthropy

During the dot-com boom, many rich people donated large sums of money through "venture philanthropy"; the idea was to invest in social and ethical causes with the same accountability and management as venture capitalists do with seed capital. Six Sigma can help take the charity portfolio concept to the next level. By using scorecard measures of charitable goals—pulling families out of poverty or curing cancer—together with sophisticated analyses of root causes, Six Sigma can significantly improve the performance of charitable investments.

Experts who have applied good analytical techniques identical to what Six Sigma would recommend have shown early successes in driving better charitable work. For example, *The Economist* reports that health care in poor countries is often directed toward rich people's diseases that aren't the biggest root cause of death and suffering (*Economist*, 2002). To counter this problem, researchers in Tanzania defined the problem as preventing infant mortality, and measured and analyzed that health resources were unrelated to the deaths of Tanzanian infants. By redirecting 80 cents per person per year toward the biggest root-cause diseases (improved step of DMAIC), they were able to reduce infant mortality by a remarkable 28 percent in one single year. By using these and other Six Sigma techniques to get at the root cause of human suffering, rather than just addressing the symptoms, philanthropic intentions can have bigger impacts.

Further, philanthropy can be improved by using Six Sigma within charitable organizations as well as by individuals and foundations that invest across a variety of charities and manage them as a portfolio. It's not new to manage investments in charities that have low overhead, a high percentage of dollars going toward the goal, and high success rates. What is rare, however, is to use models that allow you to predict where to invest next when reviewing a competing set of charities. By using the statistical concept of confidence interval, Bayesian decision making, and simulations (i.e., Monte Carlo), donors can better decide which charities convert dollars into aide most effectively by examining the variability of their past performance and expectations about future performance.

The charity Trickle Up is an interesting example of this. Trickle Up, which provides training and grants to families in abject poverty, has been remarkably successful in creating better standards of living. Since 1979, Trickle Up has created more than 100,000 entrepreneurs from the poorest of the poor around the world; people who are so poor that no bank would lend them startup capital. The results of Trickle Up's program are impressive—in 2001, 91 percent of the participants sustained ongoing businesses, with 78 percent expanding (Trickle Up, 2001, p. 2).

Trickle Up's process starts with general business education, using market analysis to select an appropriate business, and each entrepreneur grows a business through sweat equity. Entrepreneurs successful at achieving business goals are rewarded with a second infusion of startup capital—typically $50 U.S.

Some of Trickle Up's clients have Web sites and sell their goods around the globe. If some of the simpler Six Sigma techniques were used in these businesses—such as process mapping, voice of the customer, and basic measurements—these businesses could reach even better levels of performance. We're confident that as these techniques are used more extensively by philanthropic investors and recipients alike, organizations with a longstanding track record, such as Trickle Up, can be even more effective at delivering charity.

Chapter 4

Six Sigma—
Final Thoughts

Motorola invented Six Sigma, and we have had many years to reflect on our past successes and failures. What began as a way to reduce defects has become an overall business improvement framework that marries the scientific method with business acumen. Over the years, we've gained several key insights. We've discovered that the formula for Six Sigma success involves Aligning projects and executives around the metrics and projects that matter, Mobilizing them in action learning Black Belt teams, Accelerating their progress, and Governing the sustained results. We're confident that Six Sigma's past history of solid results gives it a foundation on which to grow. The use of scientific methods and applications for solving a wide range of organizational problems is just beginning to show promise. While no one can forecast the future perfectly, we've highlighted what we believe are the most compelling and likely directions. We're quite certain the future of Six Sigma is very bright.

Bibliography

Amabile, T. (1996). *Creativity in Context.* Boulder: Westview Press.

The American Banker (2002, August 28). Celebrated Six Sigma Has Its Critics, Too.

Barney, M. F. (2002). Measuring ROI in Corporate Universities: Death of the Student Day and Birth of Human Capital. In Allen, M. (ed.), *The Corporate University Handbook.* New York: American Management Association

Barney, M. F. (2001, October). Macro, Meso, Micro: Human Capital. *The Industrial-Organizational Psy-*

chologist. *http://www.siop.org/tip/backissues/*
TipOct01/11barney.htm

Copeland, T. and Antikarov, V. (2001). *Real Options: A Practitioner's Guide.* New York: Texere.

DiFrancesco, J. (2002, March). Managing Human Capital as a Real Business Asset. *IHRIM Journal.*

DiFrancesco, J. and Berman, S. J. (2000, Summer). Human Productivity: The New American Frontier. *National Productivity Review.*

Economist (2002, August 17–23). Health Care in Poor Countries: Cheap Cures. vol. 364, no. 8286, pp. 13–14.

Goldratt, E. M., Cox, J. (1986). *The Goal: A Process of Ongoing Improvement.* Croton-on-Hudson, NY: North River Press.

Guastello, S. (1995). *Chaos, Catastrophe, and Human Affairs: Application of Nonlinear Dynamics to Work, Organizations, and Social Evolution.* Mahwah, NJ: Lawrence Earlbaum Associates.

Kaplan, R. S. and Norton, D. P. (1996). *The Balanced Scorecard: Translating Strategy into Action.* Boston: Harvard Business School Press.

Lev, B. (2001). *Intangibles: Management, Measurement and Reporting.* Washington, DC: Brookings Institution Press.

Lev, B. (2002, February 6). *The Reform of Corporate Reporting and Auditing.* Testimony before the House of Representatives Committee on Energy and Commerce. *http://pages.stern.nyu.edu/~blev/*

REFORMOFCORPORATEREPORTING[1].BARU CHLEV.doc

Litan, R. and Wallison, P. (2000). *The GAAP Gap: Corporate Disclosure in the Information Age.* Washington, DC: AEI-Brookings Joint Center for Regulatory Studies.

Ones, D. S., Viswesvaran, C., and Schmidt, F. L. (1993). Comprehensive Meta-analysis of Integrity Test Validities: Findings and Implications for Personnel Selection and Theories of Job Performance. *Journal of Applied Psychology* (Monograph), 78, 679–703.

Sternberg, R. J. & Lubart, T. I. (1991). An Investment Theory of Creativity and Its Development. *Human Development,* 34, 1–31.

Trickle Up (2001). *Trickle Up Program 2001 Annual Report. http://www.trickleup.org/Annual2001.pdf,* p. 2.

Index

About the Contributors

Dr. Matt Barney, the director of Six Sigma Business Improvement Group for Motorola University, has leadership experience in a variety of business improvement roles at Intel, AT&T, Lucent Technologies, and Motorola, among other companies. His current work integrates interdisciplinary ideas from Finance, Engineering, Strategy, Statistics, Information Technology, and Psychology to improve overall organizational effectiveness.

Barney has published book chapters and presented papers on topics that include human capital management, HR technology, personnel selection, and training; he also writes the "Macro, Meso, Micro" column in the quarterly journal *The Industrial-Organizational Psychologist*. The author of three U.S. patents, Barney has others pending. He serves on the advisory board of Knowledge Advisors, a training measurement technology firm, and is a member of the Academy of Management, the Society for Industrial and Organizational Psychology, and the American Psychological Society. Barney holds a B.S. in Psychology from the University of Wisconsin–Madison and a Master's and Ph.D. in Industrial-Organizational Psychology from the University of Tulsa.

Tom McCarty is the vice-president of consulting and training services for Motorola University, where he focuses on improving the business performance of Motorola's suppliers, channel partners, customers, and business alliances through performance consulting, process consulting, and business improvement consulting. Previously, McCarty served as director of global products and systems education for Motorola's Land Mobile Products Sector, with responsibility for design, delivery, and marketing of technical training for customers, and as group vice-president of training for Motorola's U.S. Distribution Group, with responsibility for sales and customer support training. He also has 14 years of direct sales and sales management experience. McCarty recently served on the board of directors of the Professional Society for Sales and Marketing Training and on the board of trustees for the University of Syracuse Graduate School of Sales and Marketing. He earned his undergraduate degree in Business Administration from the University of Kentucky and his M.B.A. from Southern Illinois University.

Ed Bales, one of the founders of Motorola University, retired in 1997 after more than 33 years with the company. A leader in developing business/education partnerships focused on the systemic transformation of learning and teaching, Bales served as director of education, External Systems, at the time of his retirement. Between 1985 and 1990, Bales managed the design, development, and delivery of all Motorola University programs in his role as Motorola University's director of operations. His responsibility also included all North American Operations of the University

Bales recently resigned as the U.S. representative to and vice-chairman of the education committee of the business industry advisory committee of the Organization for Economic Cooperation and Development, based in Paris, France; in this capacity Bales developed several publications that examined global change in the education system. A member of the board of trustees of the Society of Actuaries Foundation and the Ray Graham Association for People with Disabilities, Bales has served on the National Conference Board Education Committee, the National Alliance of Business business/policy and education committees, the National Science Foundation education advisory committee, the National Association of School Boards Foundation, the National Academy of Sciences corporate council on math and science education and roundtable on work, learning, and assessment. His career at Motorola also included positions in product engineering, marketing, and national sales management.

Alejandro Reyes, director of leadership and performance education for Motorola University, has responsibility for the design, development, and implementation of leadership education solutions for the corporation. Reyes directly oversees 10 courses as well as six major systems and services for a target audience that includes more than 31,000 executives, directors, middle managers, and new managers worldwide.

Reyes has researched quality in education and is author of several publications in the fields of education, distance learning, and technology management. He also received Mexico's 1992 Dana Technology Prize and wrote *Quality Techniques and Models in the Classroom,* a book used for faculty development programs in Mexico and Latin America. Reyes holds a Master's of Science in Manufacturing Systems and Automation from Monterrey Institute of Technology (ITESM), Mexico, and an Industrial Engineering degree from Autonomous Metropolitan University, Mexico City.

Carey Dassatti is the corporate vice-president and director of Leadership Supply Operations. Dassatti joined Motorola in 1989 and has led Human Resource teams in organizational effectiveness. For the last two years, he has directed Leadership Supply Operations, developing processes that attract, upgrade, and retain leaders to meet current and future needs as well as developing processes for world-class general managers and individuals to lead critical staff functions.

He was an executive recruiter for nine years and gained manufacturing operations experience while at Everyready Battery. A native of Massachusetts and a graduate of Rensselaer Polytechnic Institute in Troy, New York, Dassatti holds both a Bachelor of Science in Manufacturing Management and an M.B.A. with a concentration in Behavioral Science.